# Hot Knots

Fresh Macramé Ideas for Jewelry, Home, and Fashion

First edition for North America and the Philippines published in 2015
by Barron's Educational Series, Inc.

Copyright 2015 © RotoVision SA, Sheridan House, 114 Western
Road, Hove, East Sussex BN3 1DD, England

*All inquiries should be addressed to:*
Barron's Educational Series, Inc.
250 Wireless Boulevard
Hauppauge, New York 11788
www.barronseduc.com

Publisher: Mark Searle
Editorial Director: Isheeta Mustafi
Commissioning Editor: Jacqueline Ford
Editor: Lyn Coutts
Assistant Editor: Tamsin Richardson
Design concept: Lucy Smith
Page layout: JC Lanaway
Cover design: Michelle Rowlandson
Illustrator: Rob Brandt
Photography: Neal Grundy

ISBN: 978-1-4380-0565-2

Library of Congress Control Number: 2014956306

Printed in China

9 8 7 6 5 4 3 2 1

Cover image credits
Front cover (clockwise from top left): Bangles by Jessica Eden of
BohemEden; Market bag by Jo Abellera of KKIBO; Petal earrings by Alessia
Iorio of Knotted World; Macramé edged wrap by Claudia Rosillo of
Texturable, photo by Missgong; Plant hanger by Milenka Osen and Georgie
Swift of TMOD; Upper arm bracelet by Erica Fransson of Lillagunilla.
Back cover (from left to right): Drop earrings by Kirri-Mae Sampson of
KIRRI-MAdE; Towel rail by Emma Radke of The Throwbackdaze; Friendship
bracelet by Anastasia Khazyrbekava of Thread Design Studio.
Opposite: Cord bracelet by Tanya Aguiñiga.

# Hot Knots

## Fresh Macramé Ideas for Jewelry, Home, and Fashion

Kat Hartmann

BARRON'S

# Contents

# Introduction

Macramé has made a fashion and design resurgence. No longer relegated to dusty back shelves of thrift stores and vintage fairs; handmade wall hangings, plant hangers, clutches, and custom pieces can be seen adorning racks in high-fashion stores in Los Angeles and New York, and the walls and lobbies of boutique hotels in London, Shanghai, Sydney, and beyond.

In cities such as Melbourne, Australia, communities of macramé crafters and designers have sprung up. Together, they collaborate in shared studio spaces and push the boundaries of the craft by creating everything from one-of-a-kind, statement piece necklaces to large-scale installations that adorn VIP spaces at international events like the Australian Open tennis tournament.

Macramé designers are popping up everywhere, setting up stalls at local design markets, and trading their wares internationally on Etsy.com. From the classic to the contemporary, the cutting edge to the kitsch, macramé artists and designers are changing people's preconceived notions of the craft by fusing traditional knotting techniques with new materials.

The designers featured in this book have a unique take on this craft and it is uncompromisingly displayed in their wares. Some work in collaborative inner-city studios, while others work solo from home workspaces overlooking the ocean. The one thing they have in common is a passion for this ancient craft and an ability to reinvent and revitalize it through the works they create.

**Monkey's fist ornament** *page 64*

**Picot-edged bookmark** *page 48*

## DIFFICULTY RATING
The projects and knots are rated on each page as follows:

 Easy

Medium

Difficult

# How to Use This Book

## DEVELOP YOUR KNOTTING SKILLS, CHAPTER BY CHAPTER

Each chapter begins with a tutorial for a new knot. Though the knot may feature predominantly in the project that follows, note that most projects in this book use more than one knot so always check the "Other knots used" box at the beginning to ensure you've practiced all the knots needed. Each knot and project also comes with a difficulty rating (shown opposite)—easy, medium, or difficult— to let you know how complicated they are.

Remember that these knots are just suggestions. Once you've learned all the basic knots featured you may want to mix things up a bit, so at the end of each chapter we've given you a little bit of inspiration for what your next step could be.

## DIY PROJECTS

Once you have mastered the knots, the DIY projects are the next step. Each project has been handpicked and presented by one of our featured macramé designers. Some projects are original, one-of-a-kind custom works crafted by the designers and not available anywhere else. Others are vintage items, reinvented especially for this book. Some feature one or two specific knots, and others a combination of four or five. It is worth making sure you have mastered all the knots featured in a project before you begin.

*Cord bracelet* page 98

*Towel rack* page 60

# Tools

There are a number of tools you will need to make macramé work easier.

**Workspace** Some crafters find it easier to work from a specific work table, while others prefer to work wherever the mood takes them. If you choose the former, think about the location, the lighting, and the size of the projects you plan to work on.

**Working board** Normally made from foam, working boards in a range of sizes can be purchased from most craft stores. If you have storage space, a larger working board is better as you can work a variety of project types on it. Alternatively, there are plenty of "how to" instructions for making your own that can be found through a quick online search.

**Swivel/working hook** If you are planning on making a few plant hangers you may want to consider installing a swivel or working hook in your workspace. A swivel hook should be mounted from the ceiling after consulting with a tradesman or a member of staff at a hardware store. A working hook can be mounted directly to a wall.

**Tying tool** This tool is used for the monkey's fist knot (see page 66), and it can be purchased at most craft stores. It is also fairly easy to make and "how to" instructions can be found by searching online.

**Masking/painter's tape** This can be purchased from any craft or hardware store. It is often used to seal the ends of rope or cord or to seal off sections of macramé or when painting to ensure clean lines.

**Paintbrush** The project you are working on will dictate the brush required. Flat set ends on brushes are useful for precise lines or edges.

**Needle-nosed pliers** This is a fairly essential item if you are working on any of the jewelry projects in this book. Pliers can be purchased online or at a craft or hardware store.

**Pins** Simple sewing pins will do the job for most projects, but T-pins are also useful.

**Fabric glue** This is used for securing or sealing cord ends.

**Cords** Popular cords and ropes used in macramé include jute, T-shirt yarn, paracord, nylon, hemp, leather, and cotton. Micro projects, like earrings, are best done with a soft flexible cord that is less than $1/8$ in (2–3 mm) in diameter. Braided cords unravel less easily than twisted, and nylon cords are an excellent choice when starting out as mistakes are easier to untie.

**Scissors** Any pair of sewing scissors will do as long as they are sharp.

**Dowel** This cylindrical, wooden rod is used in some macramé projects, such as wall hangings. Some projects in this book call for a dowel of specific length and diameter, while others allow for a more creative choice.

# Knotting essentials

The overhand knot is the most basic knot in macramé. Here is how to tie it: You will need a piece of cord no shorter than 4 in (10 cm) in length.

1: With the cord horizontal and straight, make a loop by crossing the right end over the left end. Feed the right end up through the loop.

2: Pull both ends of the cord to secure the overhand knot.

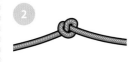

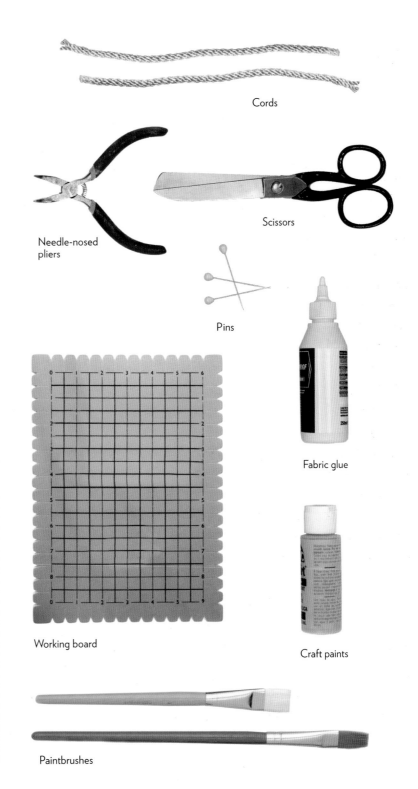

Cords

Needle-nosed pliers

Scissors

Pins

Working board

Fabric glue

Craft paints

Paintbrushes

# The Projects

# Key Chain

## Half Knot

Charlene Spiteri's interest in rope and cord started when she was taught the basics by her mother. After completing school in the late 1990s, she began a degree in textile design where she majored in weaving. An active curiosity in macramé followed shortly thereafter. In 2006, Spiteri started a design company, Warp & Weft, and began applying traditional macramé techniques to contemporary pieces. What attracted Spiteri to macramé? "I love how you can start with just a selection of cords in various colors and a design idea and you can conjure up an amazing piece," she says.

### ABOUT THE KEY CHAIN

For anyone new to macramé, the key chain is an excellent project to start with. It's simple and quick and a great way to practice your skills. Many people choose projects like this to practice other knots on as well as it's small enough for you to start over if you make a mistake.

### ABOUT THE HALF KNOT

The half knot is the foundation for a range of other knots, including the square knot (see page 44), the square knot sinnet (see page 62), and the spiral knot (which is just a series of half knots) that is used in this chapter's DIY project. The half knot is easy to learn, so it is a great one to master early. A half knot provides sufficient interest that it can feature in netted works like wall hangings and macramé curtains, and in multi-knot pieces, such as plant hangers or hanging vases.

### You will need

- A 5-in (12-cm) length of dowel that is secured to your work surface or a working board

- Three pieces of cord 56 in (142 cm), 20 in (51 cm), and 12 in (30 cm) in length

- A 1½-in (4-cm) key chain ring

- A small bead with a maximum outer diameter of 1 in (2.5 cm)

- Scissors

### Other knots used

- Lark's head knot, page 18

- Wrap knot, page 38

### Tip

As this key chain will be handled regularly, it is a good idea to make it using a man-made fiber like nylon. It will wash easily and remain color-fast.

# How to Tie a Half Knot

1: Secure two 5-in (12-cm) lengths of cord to the dowel using a lark's head knot (see page 18). Take the left cord over the two cords in the center and then under the right working cord. Some macramé enthusiasts know this as the C-step because of the "C" made by the cord.

2: Take the right cord under the two cords in the center, making a "D," up through the center of the "C," and over the left cord. Pull on both cords gently to secure the knot.

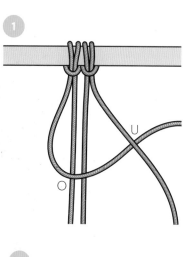

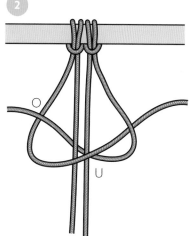

# How to Make the Key Chain

1: Secure the key chain ring to a dowel or working board. Thread 8 in (20 cm) of the two longest cords through the ring and tie a lark's head knot (see page 18). You should now have four strands on the dowel. Arrange the cords so that two strands are longer and these should be on the far left and far right. The two shorter cords will be in the center.

2: Tie a half knot. Tie a second half knot to begin creating a spiral knot. Continue to tie half knots until the spiral knot is 1½ in (4 cm) in length.

3: Thread the bead onto the shorter cords until it reaches the spiral knot. Secure the bead in place with a half knot tied using the outer cords. Continue to tie half knots for a further 1½ in (4 cm).

4: Secure the threads with a wrap knot (see page 38) using the 12 in (30 cm) length of cord.

5: Trim any loose and uneven ends.

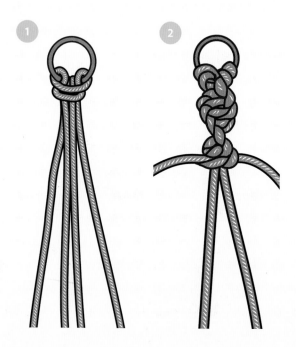

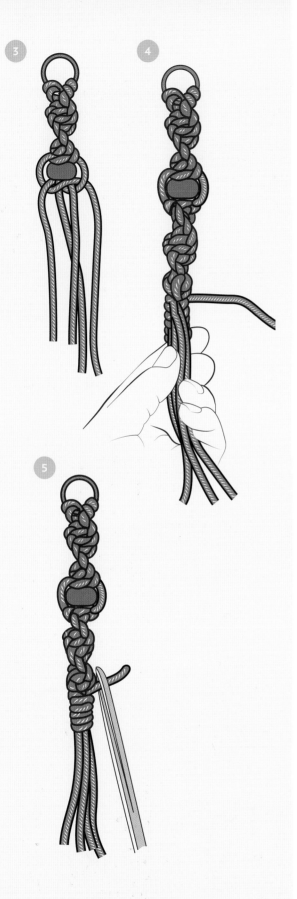

## Another Idea to Try

### Bangles

Tying half knots in one direction creates a tactile spiral effect. Here, Jessica Eden of BohemEden has used this technique to create these beautiful, eye-catching bangles (below). Making them in a variety of bright colors helps them stand out as statement pieces of jewelry. Experiment with the colors; using three tones of one color will create complementary, coordinating bangles, while three contrasting colors can be more striking.

# Dream Catcher

*by* EMILIA LORENA

## Lark's Head Knot

Australian crafter and small business owner, Emilia Lorena, left a successful job in the city when the call of coastal-town life became too strong. "At 20 I was working 14-hour-days in a creative marketing agency for multimillion dollar companies and loving every minute of it, but there was something missing," she says.

### ABOUT THE DREAM CATCHER

Though dream catchers tend to be one of the more traditional macramé items you can create it continues to be a popular item for crafters to make, not least because it's a great way to show off some beautifully decorative knots. What's great about this project is that it shows you how a combination of some of the simplest macramé knots can result in something that looks incredibly detailed and elaborate.

### ABOUT THE LARK'S HEAD KNOT

The lark's head knot is one of the simplest and most commonly used knots in macramé. It is often the starting point for many pieces—like the dream catcher project in this chapter—as it is a useful way of attaching your working cords to a holding cord. However, it can also be used as a decorative knot in its own right, as in the picot-edged bookmark project on page 48.

## You will need

- Large, flat open surface on which to work

- Ten pieces of $\frac{1}{4}$-in (6-mm) nylon cord 10 ft (310 cm) in length

- Two metal rings: one 2 in (5 cm) in diameter, the other 8 in (20 cm) in diameter

- Sharp scissors

## Tip

To prevent very long cords tangling as you're working, wind each cord loosely around your palm, slip it off your hand and secure the bundle with a rubber band. Release some of the cord as you work and re-secure with the band.

# How to Tie a Lark's Head Knot

1: Take a length of cord, about 12 in (30 cm) in length, and fold it in half, ensuring the ends of the cord are even. Pin a short holding cord—about 4 in (10 cm)—to your working board. Lay the folded cord (working cord) over the holding cord with the loop above the holding cord. You can replace the holding cord with a dowel, ring, or any other item you wish to attach your project to.

2: Fold the loop down behind the holding cord. Feed the two free ends of the working cord through the loop and pull.

3: When all the cord has passed through the loop, pull to set the lark's head knot.

You can also create a reverse lark's head knot by bringing the loop of folded cord under the top of the holding cord, then tucking the free ends through the loop.

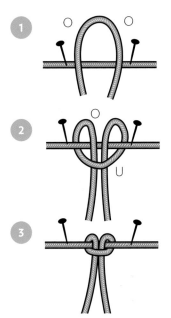

# How to Make the Dream Catcher

1: Fold each of your ten cords in half, and then adjust to make one side of each folded cord 8 in (20 cm) longer than the other. Tie each folded cord to the 2-in (5-cm) ring using lark's head knots.

2: Take two cords from one of the lark's head knots, and using the longer cord as the working cord, wrap it around the shorter cord (holding cord) and tuck it through to tighten. Repeat this to create a spiral 3 in (8 cm) long.

3: Repeat step 2 for the remaining nine pairs of working cords. You should end up with ten half knot spirals in total.

4: Lay the 8-in (20-cm) ring on a large, flat surface. Place the smaller ring and cords in the center, spreading the cords neatly and evenly around and on top of the larger ring, and then out across the work surface.

5: Attach each of the ten pairs of working cords to the outer ring, evenly spaced around the circumference, with a lark's head knot. Pull tight to secure. Use a piece of thread to mark one lark's head knot as the "top" of your ring. There should be 20 working cords extending out from the larger metal hoop.

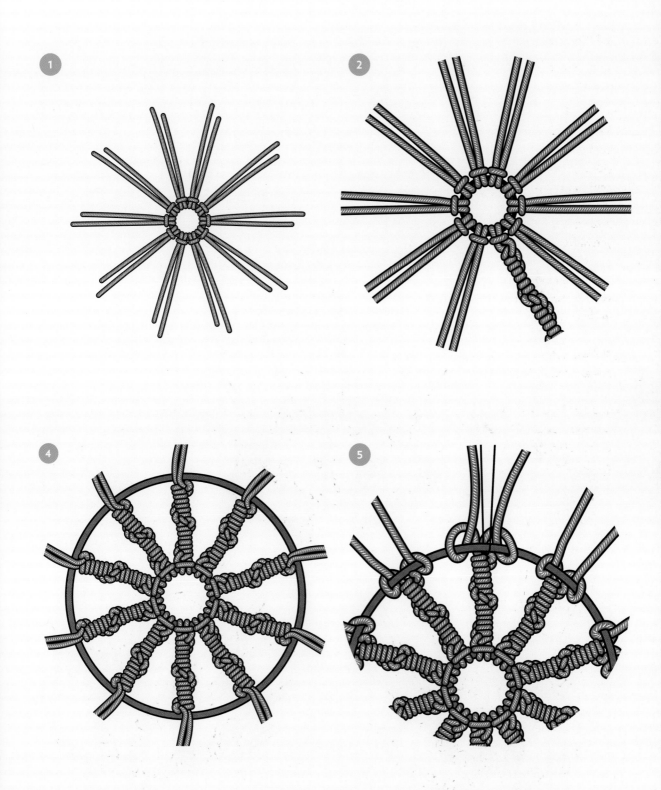

# How to Make the Dream Catcher

6: At the "top" knot, take one working cord under and back around the ring, through the loop you created. Pull tight. Repeat with all the remaining strands.

7: Starting at the "top" again, repeat steps 5 and 6. The working cord on the left will run along the ring toward the next lark's head knot on the left; the one on the right will work toward the next lark's knot on the right. These knots should cover the bare sections of the ring. There should be three cords to the left and to the right of "top."

8: Take the cord to the left of the "top" and run it under the two cords to its left, and attach to the ring with a lark's head knot. Do the same with the other two cords on the right, starting with the cord nearest the "top." Repeat this with the three cords to the right of "top."

9. Repeat step 8, gathering in more cords as you progress left and right of the "top" until the outer ring is covered in knots. Trim cord ends.

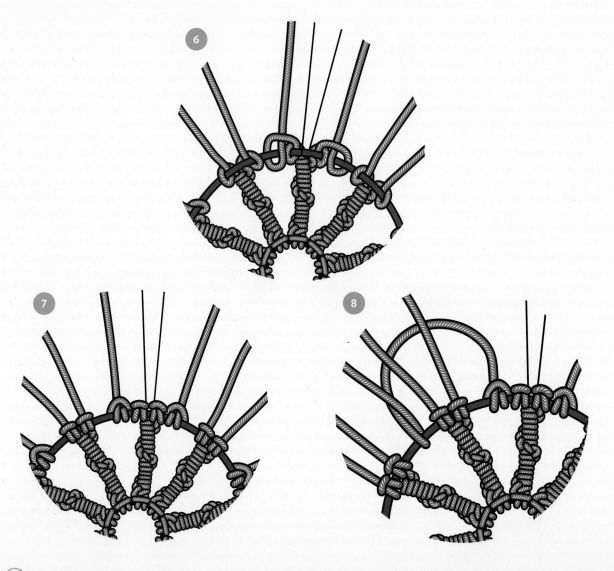

# Other Ideas to Try

## Baby swing

Although it seems a very simple knot, this baby swing (left) by Paolo Prosperio of the Hang A Hammock Collective shows how you can utilize the lark's head knot in a beautifully decorative way. Using a complementary color palette of greens and cream, Prosperio has dressed up this swing by using lark's head knots to not only conceal the wooden framework, but also make it more playful, tactile, and cozy.

## Metal and beaded ring

Little jewelry elements such as pendants lend themselves to using the lark's head knot. Attach your cords to the metal pieces using the lark's head knot and you can then choose to add more decorative knots or even just attach a few more beads to create a singular statement piece such as this ring created by Julie Comtois (right), owner of the Etsy shop, Creations Mariposa.

# Drop Earrings

*by* KIRRI-MAE SAMPSON

## Half Hitch Knot

Kirri-Mae Sampson dreams up all her design ideas from her at-times cluttered and chaotic home studio in Melbourne, Australia. Her almost-eponymously named resin and macramé range, KIRRI-MAdE, is colorful and undeniably original.

### ABOUT THE DROP EARRINGS ⑤ ⑤

This is one of the most exciting applications of modern macramé; using traditional knotting techniques to make delicate one of a kind pieces of beautiful jewelry. These earrings look detailed but are quite simple once you get the hang of the half hitch knot. Though this project uses one single color, you could try the same pattern using two or more colors.

### ABOUT THE HALF HITCH KNOT ⑤

The half hitch knot is the foundation for most of the knots featured in this book. Used on its own, it is not a particularly decorative or stable knot, but when tied twice it becomes the much more widely used double half hitch, or clove hitch, knot. It should be mastered as a single half hitch before attempting any other hitch-based knots.

## You will need

- Fine cord cut into 40 pieces, each 40 in (1 m) in length

- Two 5/8 in (16 mm) jump rings

- Working board

- Sewing pins or T-pins

- Four small metal rings 3/16 in (5 mm) in diameter

- Two French hook earring wires

- Scissors

## Other knots used

- Lark's head knot, page 18

- Square knot, page 44

- Double half hitch knot, page 72

## Tip

When learning a new knot, it is fine to practice with leftover pieces of knitting or crocheting yarn, but it is not recommended that these yarns be used in finished pieces as they can stretch.

## How to Tie a Half Hitch Knot

1: Place a 3-in (8-cm) long cord vertically on the working board. This is the working cord.

2: Lay another 3-in (8-cm) long cord horizontally across the top end of the working cord. This is the holding cord. Pin the ends of the holding cord firmly in place.

3: Take the lower end of the working cord up and over the front of the holding cord, and then behind and under the holding cord and over the working cord. Pull to tighten this half hitch knot.

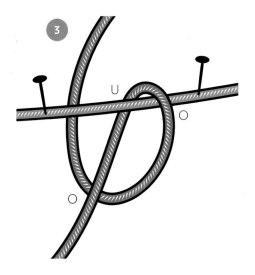

## How to Make the Earrings

1: Anchor the center of 20 lengths of the cord onto each of the large jump rings using lark's head knots (see page 18). Once the cords are attached, pin or tie the jump rings securely to the working board. There will be 40 cords hanging from each jump ring.

2: Start with the first two cords on the left of the first jump ring and work to the right. Using the second cord as the working cord, tie a half hitch onto the cord on the extreme left (the holding cord). Repeat to tie a double half hitch knot (see page 72). Repeat using cords 3 to 20 to tie double half hitch knots onto the holding cord. Repeat on the second jump ring.

3: Repeat step 2 on the first jump ring using the last cord (cord 40) as the holding cord. The working cords are to its left (cords 39 to 21). Tie double half hitch knots on the holding cord, working clockwise. Repeat on the second jump ring.

4: Repeat steps 2–3 on both jump rings to create a second row of double half hitch knots. You should now have two rows on each ring that start top left and right and move down to the bottom. To join the two "halves" on each ring, tie two half hitch knots onto the left holding cord using the last working cord on the right. Repeat tying two half hitch knots onto the right holding cord using the last working cord on the left.

# How to Make the Earrings

5: You are now ready to start the final row of double half hitch knots. Repeat steps 2–3 on the first jump ring, *but* as each double half hitch knot is tied, preceding cords are collected to become holding cords for the next knot. For example, when the first double half hitch knot is tied there is one holding cord; for the second knot, two holding cords; and so on. As before, work from top left downward and then from top right downward. As more cords are added to each knot, the knots bulk out as the row progresses.

6: Smooth the gathered cords at the bottom to create a fringe. Repeat steps 5–6 on the second jump ring.

7: Take the last working cord on the left and on the right of one of the jump rings, and tie together with a square

knot (see page 44) around the gathered cords. Tie two or three more square knots using the same two cords to ensure the piece is secure. Repeat for the second jump ring. Un-pin the rings from working board.

8: Divide the gathered cords—19 in one group, 19 in the other—and tie a double overhand knot (see page 9) at the point where the two groups of cord divide using the two cords that tied the square knots. This further secures the piece and also plumps up the fringing. Repeat on the second jump ring. Attach two small rings and an earring hook to each large jump ring. Evenly trim the ends of the fringe to your chosen length.

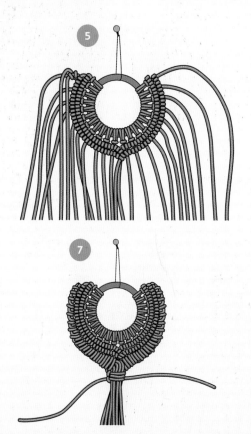

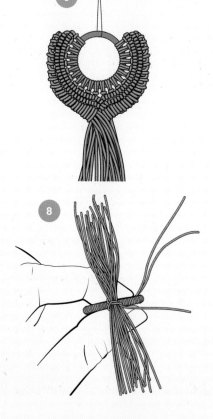

# Another Idea to Try

## Making delicate items

The half hitch knot is the perfect knot to use when making intricate, delicate items, such as these barefoot sandals by Yuli Fitie (below). The combination of fine cord, detailed knotting, and some well thought out beading in complementary colors makes for a sophisticated, yet carefree look. The fine cord and delicate knotting used in the sandals is similar to those used in Sampson's drop earrings project, yet the end result is so very different, which goes to prove the versatility and utility of macramé. A variation on this look can also be seen on page 59.

# Phone Case

*by* ELVIRA SASSO

## Alternating Half Hitch Knot

After 42 years of teaching in the UNESCO World Heritage Site town of Matera, Italy, Elvira Sasso hung up her school hat for a life of retirement and a chance to focus on crafting. After learning macramé at an early age, from her mother, Sasso went on to master knitting, crocheting, tatting, and bobbin lace as well.

### ABOUT THE PHONE CASE

This pretty phone case comes with a strap so it can be worn over your shoulder or fastened to the inside of your bag. You can also enlarge the pattern to make a similar case for your tablet or laptop. This project uses a combination of knots so it's best to practice each one first.

### ABOUT THE ALTERNATING HALF HITCH KNOT

This knot is widely used to create handles (as is shown in this chapter's DIY project), belts, wind chimes, and other hanging items. In the alternating half hitch, both cords alternate as the working and holding cords. Once mastered, this knot can also be incorporated into the plant hanger (see page 54), to add extra interest to the longer holding ropes.

## You will need

- Working board
- Twenty pieces of $5/16$-in (8-mm) waxed cotton cord: two pieces 9 ft (2.7 m) in length, and 18 pieces $5^{1}/_{2}$ ft (1.6 m) in length, plus extra for hand sewing the seams. This material and the instructions will make a phone case 3 in x $5^{1}/_{4}$ in (8 x 13.5 cm)
- Sewing pins or T-pins
- Measuring tape
- Crochet hook
- Sewing needle with a large eye
- Scissors
- Fabric glue

## Tip

For micro-macramé, Sasso uses 3-ply C-Lon nylon thread $3/16$-in (5-mm diameter), and for larger pieces $5/16$-in (8-mm) waxed cotton cord.

## Other knots used

- Lark's head knot, page 18
- Half hitch knot, page 24
- Square knot, page 44
- Double half hitch knot, page 72
- Horizontal double half hitch knot, page 78

# How to Tie an Alternating Half Hitch Knot

1: Pin two 24-in (60-cm) cords to a working board and label the cords A and B. Take B (working cord) over and under A (holding cord) and then pull B back through and over itself. This is the first half hitch knot.

2: In this step, A becomes the working cord and B the holding cord. Bring A over and under B and then pull A back through over itself. It is the same process as step 1, but in a counterclockwise direction. This is the second half hitch knot that makes up one alternating half hitch knot.

3: Continue to alternate A and B as holding and working cords, tying a half hitch knot with one cord and then the other to gain proficiency.

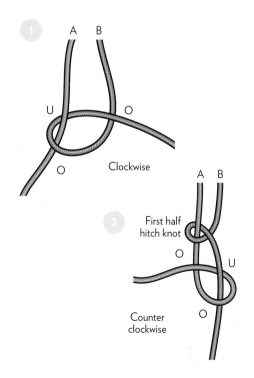

# How to Make the Phone Case

1: Find the midpoint of one of the longer 9-ft (2.7-m) cords and pin this point near the top of your working board. Lay the cords either side of the pin horizontally across the working board and secure by knotting them around pins. This is the holding cord.

2: Press a pin into the board about 1 in (2.5 cm) above the midpoint pin. (This will become the loop for the closing catch.) Fold one of the shorter 5½-ft (1.6-m) cords in half and loop it around the topmost pin. Thread the cords under the holding cord. Secure these cords—the working cords—to the holding cord with pins. Tie a half hitch knot with the working cord on the right, working to the right. Pull the knot tight.

3: Tie a second half hitch knot with the same cord to make a double half hitch knot (see page 72). Pull the knot tight.

4: Tie a double half hitch knot with the working cord on the left, working to the left. Pull to set the knots.

5: Take another one of the shorter cords and fold it in half. Thread this midpoint to the right of the first knots tied and under the holding cord so that the loop is at the top. Attach this cord to the holding cord using a lark's head knot (see page 18). Pull tightly.

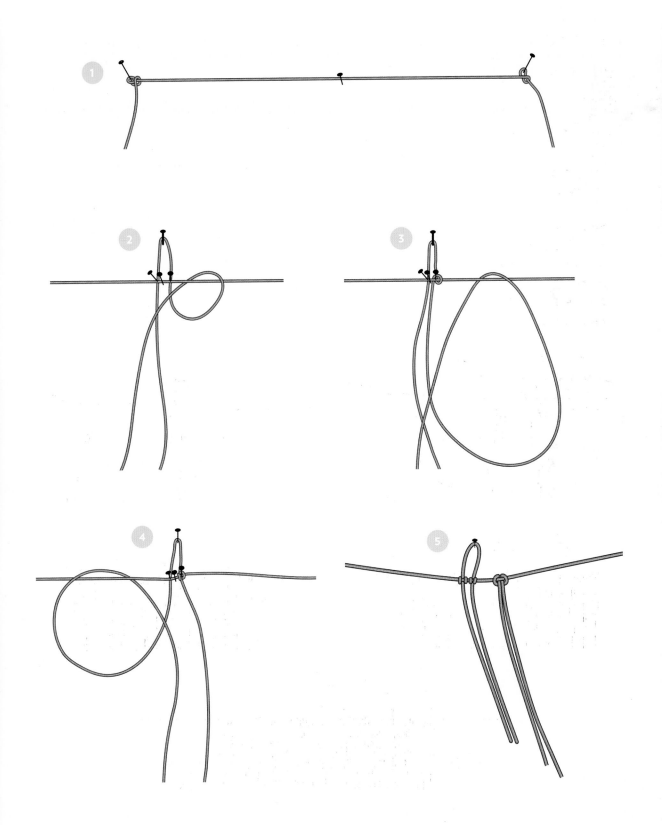

# How to Make the Phone Case

6: Using the cord furthest to the right, tie a half hitch knot (see step 1 of the alternating half hitch knot on page 30) onto the holding cord. This knot will sit to the right of the cord. Pull to secure.

7: Using the cord second from right, tie a half hitch knot, working left, onto the holding cord.

8: Repeat steps 5–7 to attach the midpoints of seven further shorter cords to the right of the midpoint, eight working cords to the left of the midpoint, and one in the center of the looped cord. In total, there will be 18 pairs of cords (36 working cords) on the holding cord.

9: Tie a row of square knots (see page 44) across all the working cords, using cords 1 and 4, 5 and 8, 9 and 12, 13 and 16, 17 and 20, 21 and 24, 25 and 28, 29 and 32, and 33 and 36 as the working cords and the others as filler cords.

10: Pin the two outermost cords on the left and on the right out of the way. Repeat step 9 to tie a second row of square knots on the remaining 16 pairs of working cords.

11: Tie an alternating half hitch knot (see steps 1–3 of alternating half hitch knot on page 30) on the two pairs of cords set aside in step 10. Start with the cord on the left of each pair as the holding cord.

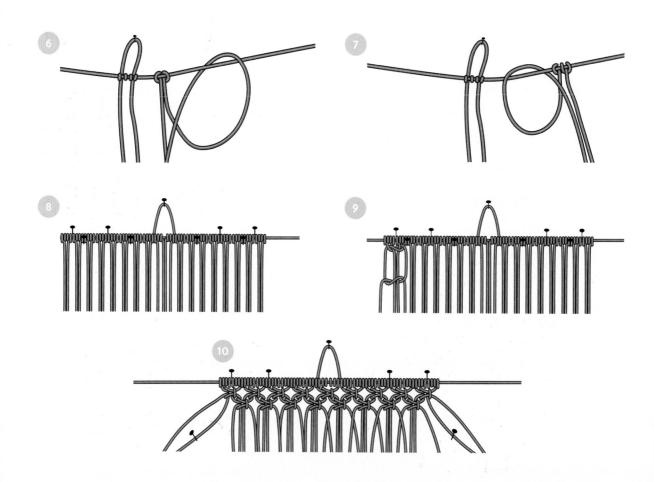

12: Tie a third row of square knots on the 18 pairs of working cords. Tie alternating half hitch knots on the two pairs of cords on the furthest left and right.

13: Repeat steps 9–11 to create rows of square knots and two alternating half hitch knots until you have tied a total of 53 rows or the macramé measures $10^{1}/_{2}$ in (26.5 cm) from holding cord to final row of knots. Pin the work as you go to help keep your knotting even.

14: Lay the remaining 9-ft (2.7-m) cord over the last row of working cords and pin to the working board. Starting with the working cords in the center, attach them to the holding cord with horizontal double half hitch knots (see page 78).

15: Continue tying horizontal double half hitch knots to attach all working cords to the holding cord.

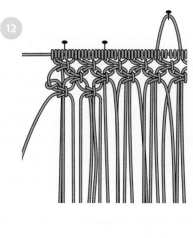

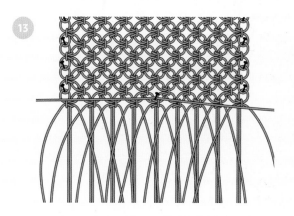

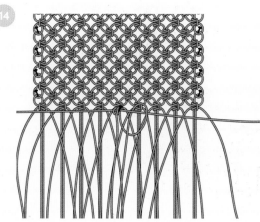

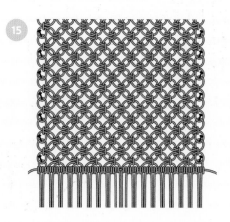

# How to Make the Phone Case

16: Unpin the work from the board. Gather the four cords in the center together and tie an overhand knot (see page 9) that sits tight against the last row of knots. Tie a second overhand knot 1 in (2.5 cm) away from the first. Feed this knot through the loop at the opposite end of the case to test for a snug fit. Trim the ends if needed.

17: Use the crochet hook to tuck each remaining working cord through the base of one of the existing knots. Trim excess cords and glue ends to secure.

18: Fold the work in half so it measures 3 in x 5¼ in (8 cm x 13.5 cm). Sew the long sides together using a sewing needle and the extra cord.

19: To make a carry handle for the case, tie a chain of alternating half hitch knots using the pairs of holding cords trailing from the top left and right of the case. Bring the two chains together and secure with an overhand knot. Trim any excess cord.

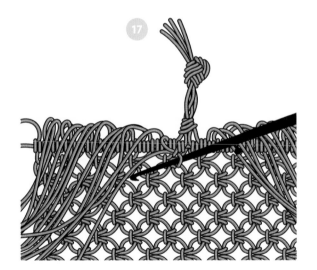

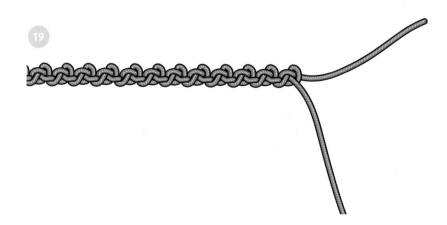

# Other Ideas to Try

## Pendant necklace

This beautiful pendant necklace by Julie Comtois (right) uses polyester waxed cord, brass beads, and a labradorite charm. The brass beads add an element of sophistication and combined with the bold green create a striking piece. Comtois always uses a sliding knot at the end of her necklaces so that the length can be adjusted.

## Using found items

This wall hanging by Sally England (left) uses cotton cord, yarn, and a found branch that combine to create a clean and modern take on traditional macramé wall hangings. England used a lark's head knot to attach the cord to the branch and then created the rest of the wall hanging with a combination of the vertical clove hitch knot and weaving techniques making this an interesting and striking hybrid of yarn craft styles.

# Plant Hanger

*by* CHARLENE SPITERI

## Wrap Knot

Charlene Spiteri endeavors to ensure that the materials used in her pieces are as sustainable as possible, sourcing them from nearby businesses when she can. However, she admits that it is not always the easiest thing to do in her homeland as "local suppliers are becoming scarce in Australia."

### ABOUT THE PLANT HANGER  🌀🌀

Plant hangers are a beautiful way to decorate your home, allowing you to use your space creatively. Hang these by a window and you can ensure your plants get plenty of sunshine. This project can also be used to create some highly effective storage around your home. Replace the planter with wicker baskets and you could use this in the kitchen or bathroom when you run out of shelf space.

### ABOUT THE WRAP KNOT  🌀

The wrap knot is not one of the showiest in macramé and is often used to finish off a work or a section of a piece, making it an important knot to master early. The wrap is usually created by combining several loose cords—and often, but not always, the ends of the cords. A wrap knot is commonly found on hanging vases and planters, and in jewelry items.

## Tip

If you are planning to make multiple hanging vases or plant hangers, mount a swivel hook from the ceiling of your workspace. This allows you to turn your piece while you work on it. Depending on the height of your ceiling you might need to customize it to suit.

## You will need

- A swivel or working hook (see Tip on this page and page 8)

- Six pieces of jute 13 ft (4 m) in length

- A metal ring 1½-in (4 cm) in diameter from which to suspend the completed plant hanger

- Four pieces of cord (in three colors) 5 ft (1.5 m) in length. If the cord is thin, use four pieces 10 ft (3 m) in length doubled over to increase thickness

- Sharp scissors

- Thin string

## Other knots used

- Lark's head knot, page 18

- Square knot sinnet, page 62

# How to Tie a Wrap Knot

1: Thread five cords 10–15 in (25–40 cm) long through a ring and fold over at their midpoint. Secure the cords with a piece of thin string tied around the gathered cords just below the ring. Make a loop out of another piece of cord about 15 in (40 cm) in length (shown here as the blue cord) by folding one end back onto itself for about 3 in (8 cm). This working cord should be left long as it will do the wrapping. Lay the working cord on top of the gathered cords with the loop sitting slightly above the gathered cords.

2: Wrap the working cord around the gathered cords, leaving the end of the looped cord free below the wrap. Begin at the bottom of the area you want to wrap and move upward–or, depending on the outcome you want, from the top downward. (In this instance the loop should be at the bottom.)

3: Once you have completed wrapping the gathered cords, feed the end of the working cord through the loop created in step 1. Pull firmly on the free end of the looped cord to ensure that the wrap knot remains secure. Trim working cords to neaten.

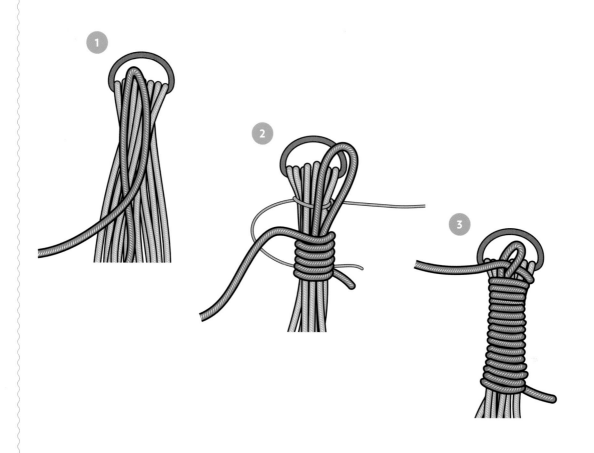

# How to Make the Plant Hanger

1: Fold the six lengths of jute in half. Gather the folded ends together, thread through the hanging ring, and tie a lark's head knot (see page 18). There will be 12 cords hanging from the ring.

2: Tie a square knot sinnet (see page 62) for 4 in (10 cm).

3: Using one length of colored cord, tie a wrap knot for 1½ in (4 cm). Repeat using two more cords in different colors, tying wrap knots for 1½ in (4 cm) and 2 in (5 cm), respectively. (The fourth colored cord will be used to tie another wrap knot to finish the plant hanger.)

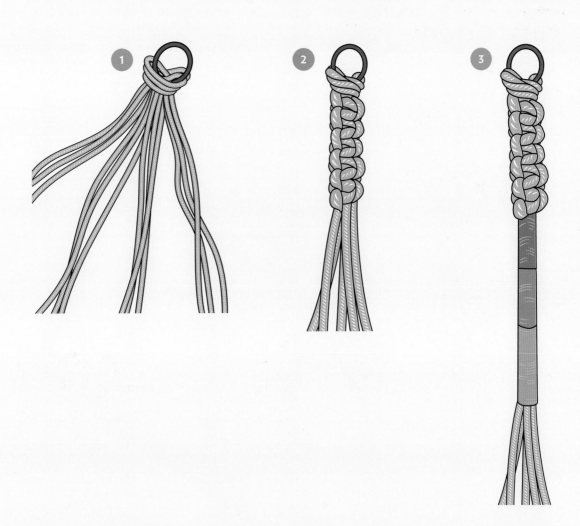

# How to Make the Plant Hanger

4: Separate the hanging cords into three groups of four. Measure 10 in (25 cm) from the base of the wrap knots down the hanging cords. Tie a square knot (see page 44) in each of the three groups of cords. Measure 2 in (5 cm) down from the base of the square knots, and bring together two cords from different groups and tie an overhand knot (see page 9). For example, the right cords of the first group are knotted to the left cords of the second group and so on until the remaining cords from the first and third groups are knotted together.

5: Measure 2–2½ in (5.5 cm) down from the base of each knot and ie another square knot using your original groups of cords from the start of step 4.

6: Gather the cords together and measure 2–2½ in (5.5 cm) down from the bases of the knots. Secure the cords with a wrap knot tied with the remaining colored cord. This knot can vary from 1–3 in (2.5–8 cm) in length, depending on the effect you want to create

7: Unravel the ends of the cords to create a frayed effect. Place a plant pot in the center of the macramé "basket."

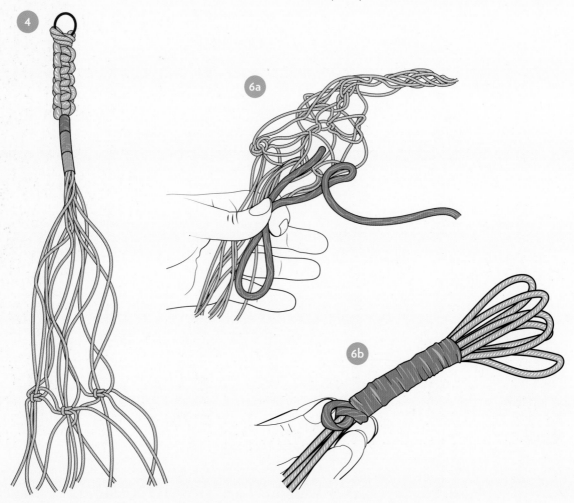

# Another Idea to Try

## Make one, then make more

Stacey Evans of Sunshine Dreaming has used half knots, wrap knots, and square knots to make this striking collection of hangers (below). The best way to get a project right is practice, practice, practice. So when you've made one plant hanger don't stop there; make more!

Experiment with the texture, color, and number of cords you use. Try incorporating different knots in varying sequences into your design. And don't be afraid to use strong colored cords; bright colors look great against neutral-colored containers.

# Headband

*by* EMILIA LORENA

## Square Knot

Designer Emilia Lorena lives a pretty idyllic life; "In my hometown, Yamba, [in New South Wales, Australia] regardless of the season, it is warm," she says. "I live in a beautiful beach house where every wall is a different color, and my work is displayed on every blank space. I have a huge balcony overlooking the ocean that I like to call my office."

### ABOUT THE HEADBAND ✪
The textured effect of the square knot makes for a very pretty headband that looks equally great in muted colors or using a combination of bold colors. These are so easy to make you could easily whip up a bunch to match all your outfits.

### ABOUT THE SQUARE KNOT ✪ ✪
The square knot is one of the most versatile of all the macramé knots and a great one to master early. It can add a decorative element to supporting ropes on plant hangers; become a bracelet or headband; or be the starting point for a one-of-a-kind wall hanging.

## Tip

Always have a range of variously sized and textured materials on hand. If you have an idea, experiment with lots of materials before settling on one. To your surprise, the design may suit a material that you least expected.

## You will need

- Five pieces of cord or T-shirt fabric 23 in (58 cm) in length (thesfiller cords) and four pieces of matching cord or T-shirt fabric 90 in (2.3 m) in length (the are working cords)

- Working board

- Measuring tape

- Sewing needle and thread in a similar color to the cord

- Sharp scissors

## Other knot used

- Square knot sinnet, page 62

# How to Tie a Square Knot

1: Secure four lengths of cord, about 24 in (60 cm) in length to your working board. Take the left cord over the two filler cords in the center and then under the cord on the right. This is known as the C-step.

2: Take the right cord under the two cords in the center, making a "D", and then bring the cord up through the center of the "C," and over the cord on the left.

3: Bring the cord now on the right (shown here as the green cord) over the center filler cords and under the cord now on the left (shown here as the red cord.)

4: Bring the left cord under the center filler cords and then up through the center of the "D" and over the right cord.

5: Pull to set the square knot. If you repeat this knot, you create a square knot sinnet (see page 62).

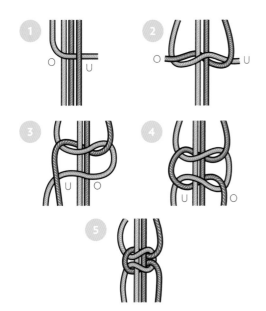

# How to Make the Headband

1: Pin one end of the five filler cords to a working board. Pin a pair of working cords to the left and to the right. Start a square knot by laying the pair of working cords on the left over the filler cords and under the working cords on the right.

2: Bring the right working cords under the filler cords and over the left working cords. Make sure this square knot sits 1¼ in (3 cm) from the ends of the filler cords.

3: Complete the square knot. Pull gently to tighten set the knot.

4: Tie more square knots until there is only 1¼ in (3 cm) of the filler cords remaining. Unpin the work.

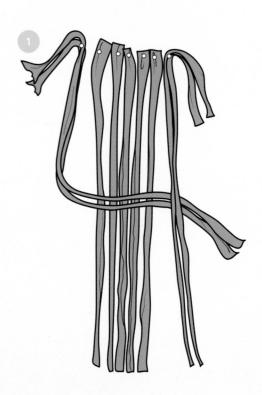

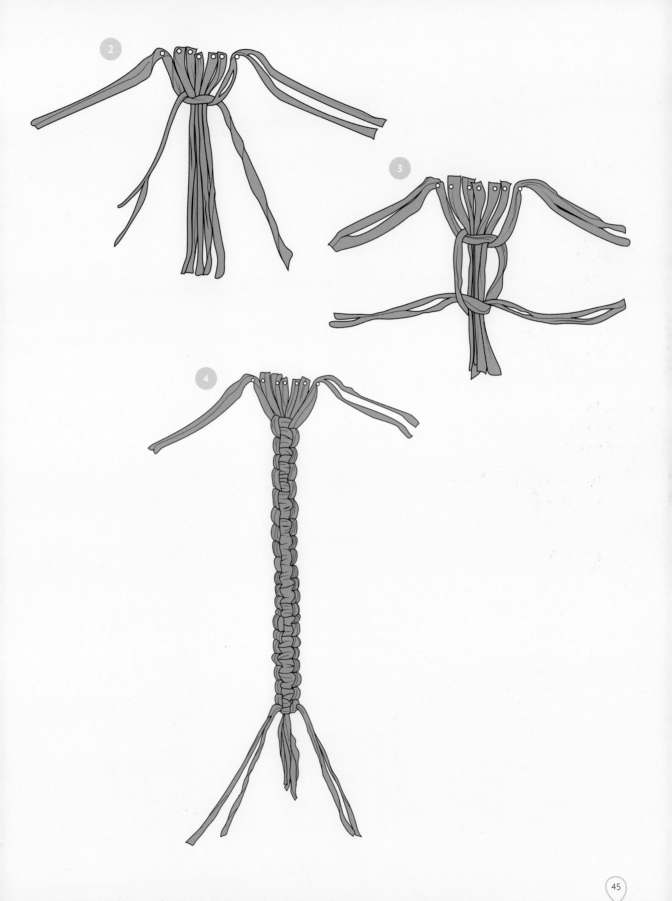

# How to Make the Headband

5: To size the headband, wrap it around your head and check where the ends of the band together. Mark where the filler cords meet for a comfortable fit. Remove from your head. With the headband folded in half, match up corresponding filler cords and align the fitting marks. Gather working cords to each side.

6: Take the first pair of filler cords. Sew them together along the fitting marks, keeping the stitches and cords flat. The stitching will not be visible. Repeat for the remaining filler cords. Trim excess material beyond the stitches. The headband is now a completed circle.

7: Using your working cords, continue to tie square knots the rest of the way around the band until you meet the first square knot tied on the headband.

8: Once you are satisfied with the stretchiness and the tension, discreetly weave the remaining working cords into the headband and trim if necessary.

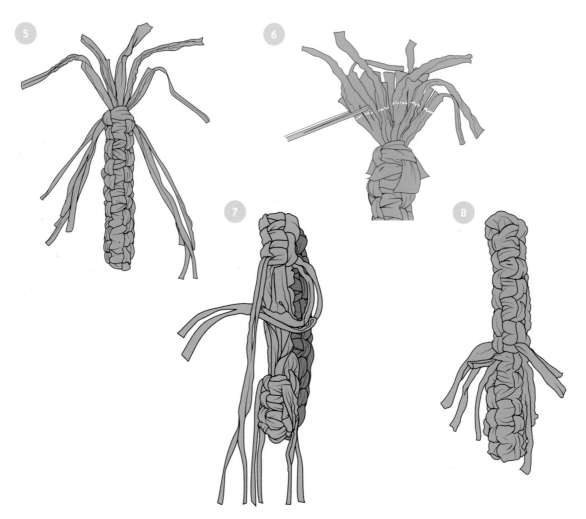

# Other Ideas to Try

## Bead-jeweled

It is really easy to jazz up your square knots by adding beading. Michelle Larson of Beso del Corazon included antique brass beads and green agate in her anklet (right) to make it simple yet chic. The brass beads add a beautiful, shiny contrast to the more muted colors of the green-gray. You can use a variety of different sized beads or keep your beads uniform, whatever strikes your fancy. Don't just stop at beads—how about including pendants, vintage charms, or found items like shells and sea glass?

## Including unusual objects

The beauty of working with macramé is that, while it can be used to make classic pieces like the anklet (above), it is also perfect for more casual jewelry too. Erica Fransson of Lillagunilla made this boho-chic upper arm bracelet (left) using a combination of the lark's head, double half hitch, and square knots. The combination of different knots helps add interest to the bracelet and the inclusion of beading and salt stone make it really unique. If budget is no object, turquoise or amber embellishments would be stunning, but for something more pocketbook friendly, smooth pieces of semi-opaque sea glass are a great option.

# Picot-Edged Bookmark

*by EMILIA LORENA*

## Alternating Lark's Head Knot

Emilia Lorena is drawn to the heritage associated with macramé. In particular, to the fact that the craft has survived through the ages, constantly reinventing itself across continents through the enthusiasm of new generations. "I love playing a part in creating modern macramé and hope to keep the art alive for as long as possible," says Lorena.

### ABOUT THE PICOT-EDGED BOOKMARK

Although a bookmark is such an everyday item, its shape and size lends itself perfectly to this macramé project. The alternating lark's head knot is beautifully decorative and gives this simple object a very special edge. Because the knot is slightly more complicated, this is a perfect project to practice it on, with very satisfying results that can be used as a lovely handmade present.

### ABOUT THE ALTERNATING LARK'S HEAD KNOT

The alternating lark's head knot, or lark's head sinnet, is a decorative knot that is used to add interest to bag handles or straps, belts, bookmarks, and to items of jewelry. It is a good idea to master the lark's head knot (see page 18) before you begin working with this alternating version.

## You will need

- Two pieces of cord, in different colors, 48 in (122 cm) in length
- One piece of cord 24 in (60 cm) in length (for use in the wrap knot)
- Working board
- Sewing pins or T-pins
- Sharp scissors
- A charm with eyelet
- A jump ring to attach the charm

## Other knots used

- Lark's head knot, page 18
- Wrap knot, page 38

## Tip

To make your bookmark more durable, Lorena recommends using a waxed cord for your project. This will also help the bookmark hold its shape better.

# How to Tie an Alternating Lark's Head Knot

1: Pin the midpoints of two 24 in (60 cm) cords, in different colors, to a working board. Arrange the four cords so colors alternate. The two center cords will be holding cords, and the two outer cords, working cords. Label the cords from left to right, A, B, C, and D. A and D are the working cords while B and C are the holding cords.

2: Tie the first loop of your lark's head knot (see page 18) to cords B and C with cord D. This lark's head knot will be right facing.

3: Complete the second loop of your lark's head knot to B and C with cord D. Tighten gently to set the knot flush to the top of the holding cords.

4: Tie a lark's head knot to cords B and C with cord A. This lark's head knot will be left facing.

5: Tighten gently to set the knot flush to the first knot to complete an alternating lark's head knot.

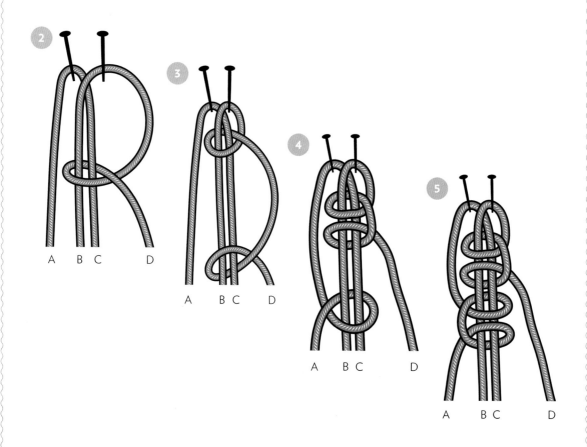

# How to Make the Picot-Edged Bookmark

1: Pin the midpoints of the two cords to the working board. Arrange the four cords so the colors alternate. Label the cords, left to right, A, B, C, and D. Tie an alternating lark's head knot on cords B and C first using cord D and then using cord A.

2: Using cord D, tie another right-facing lark's head knot on cords B and C at a point lower than the knot above. The space between these knots determines the width of the picot edging. The rule of thumb is: Leave a space twice the length of the picot width you want. Once the knot is tied, feed it gently up the holding cords to create the picot. Repeat on the right hand side using cord A to create a left-facing picot.

3: Repeat step 2 until your working cords are close to running out or the bookmark is the desired length.

4: Secure the ends with a wrap knot (see page 38) tied with the waxed cord. Trim excess cords and unpin the bookmark from the working board.

5: Thread the charm onto the jump ring, and then thread the ring onto the loop at the top of the bookmark. Close the ring and the bookmark is complete.

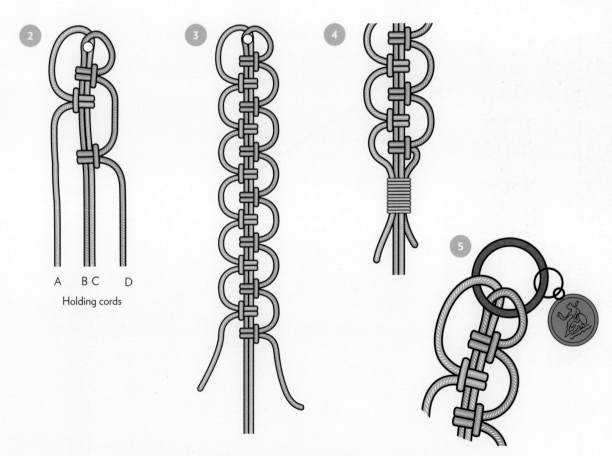

A    BC    D

Holding cords

# Other Ideas to Try

## Beaded bracelet

Mae Cleary used a picot and square knot and combined crystal beads with a blue waxed cord to make this elegant, floral bracelet (left). Bracelets are among the most common macramé items and though they vary in styles, Cleary opts for simple embellishments that really let the knots take center stage.

## Decorative straps

Laura Pifer transformed this beach top (right) with some decorative macramé straps turning it from an unremarkable outfit into something special. You could try this effect with a combination of any of the knots featured in the book—the alternating lark's head could make some really cute picot-edged straps, for example—but remember to use cords that match the fabric well so that it doesn't cause your item to buckle or twist.

## Make a classic piece

Owls are a staple of traditional macramé and retro versions can be seen everywhere, from yard sales to trendy vintage stores. But just because it's a classic piece doesn't mean you can't put your own twist on it. Laura Ayres-Selent gave her macramé owl a fresh, contemporary feel by using white cords, simple wooden beads, and understated half hitch knots (opposite).

# Beaded Plant Holder

*by* TMOD

## Berry Knot

Sydney designers Milenka Osen and Georgie Swift launched TMOD, and enjoy exploring the way in which macramé blends creativity with utility. Says Osen, "You can make something unique and functional simply from a piece of rope." The pair approach their macramé in a rather structured and practical way. After researching and sketching designs, they move on to mini prototypes, which they experiment with before committing to a full-scale design. They combine their amassed learning into creating DIY kits that can be given as gifts or used by other macramé enthusiasts.

### ABOUT THE BEADED PLANT HOLDER ⑤⑤

This is similar to the plant hanger project shown earlier in the book with the difference that this one is more muted and delicate. You could even use this pattern on thinner cords to hold smaller vases or a terrarium. Because you don't necessarily have to use thick cord for this, you can use a wide range of colors and match the project to the color scheme in your home.

### ABOUT THE BERRY KNOT ⑤⑤

The berry knot is a great way to use some of the skills learnt when practising the square knot (see page 44) and the square knot sinnet (see page 62) practice. The berry knot takes the square knot sinnet one step further, turning it into a decorative little ball. A berry knot, like a bead, can break the monotony of long, straight cords on a plant hanger, but also looks great as a statement detail on the end of a necklace.

## You will need

- A swivel hook (see page 8) or similar

- A hanging ring that is in proportion to the length of the hanger. One that is 1–2 in (2.5–5 cm) in diameter suits most hangers

- Four pieces of cord or rope 8 ft (2.5 m) in length

- Four round decorative beads with $1/3$-in (8-mm) diameter hole in center. If working with thick cords, a bigger bead with a larger hole may be needed

## Other knots used

- Lark's head knot, page 18

- Square knot, page 44

- Square knot sinnet, page 62

# How to Tie a Berry Knot

1: Fold two 24-in (60-cm) long cords, in half and attach each cord to a ring with lark's head knot (see page 18). Tie a square knot sinnet (see page 62) being careful not to tighten it right up to the ring. A minimum of five knots is needed to create a sinnet.

2: Bring the center cords over the sinnet and thread them through the gap above the sinnet and between the cords.

3: Pull down on the cords so that the sinnet curls back on itself to form a berry shape.

4: Tie a square knot (see page 44) at the base of the berry knot to secure it.

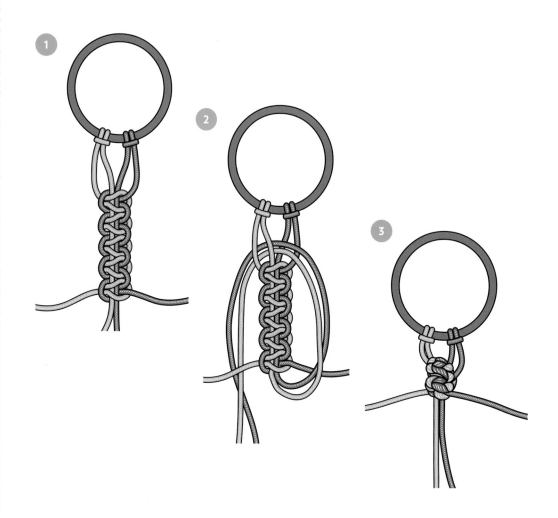

# How to Make the Beaded Plant Holder

1: Fold the cords in half and attach at the midway point to the ring with a lark's head knot (see page 18). Ensure the strings are taut before you begin tying.

2: Using the outer left and outer right cords (the working cords) tie a square knot sinnet (see page 62). Tie a berry knot following the instructions on the opposite page.

3: Gather the cords into four groups of two cords. Measure approximately 14 in (35 cm) from the base of the berry knot down the first pair of cords. Thread on a bead. Tie an overhand knot (see page 9) below the bead to keep it in place. Repeat for the remaining three pairs of cords.

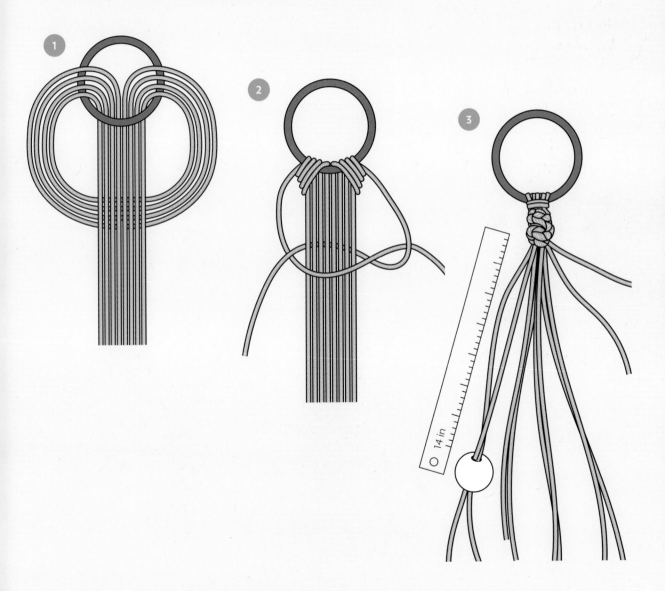

# How to Make the Beaded Plant Holder

4: Take the right cord of the first group and the left cord of the second group. Measure 2¹⁄₂ in (6.5 cm) from the base of the knots down the cords, and knot the cords together using an overhand knot. Take the right cord of the second group and the left cord of the third group, measure and then knot together. Repeat until all the cords are similarly joined and knotted.

5: Leaving 2¹⁄₂ in (6.5 cm) gap between the row of knots above, knot as instructed in step 4.

6: Measure 2¹⁄₂ in (6.5 cm) down all the cords from the second knot. Gather the cords and tie them together using a second berry knot.

7: Place the plant pot in center of the macramé "basket." The base of the plant pot will rest on the lowest berry knot. Trim ends as necessary.

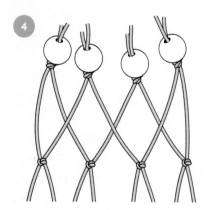

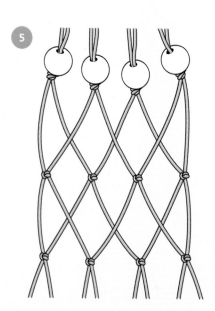

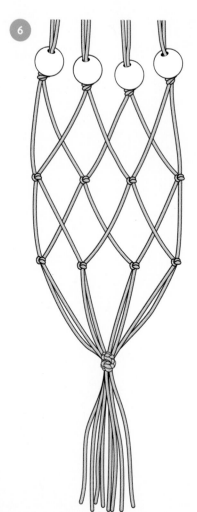

# Other Ideas to Try

## Decorative anklet

Marja and Bea Kort of Passii Sieraden combine cord and semiprecious stones to create these gorgeous sandals that look great on the beach (right). Now trending as "barefoot sandals" in the crafting world, these are the latest thing in handmade fashion and can be used as anklets but are a great way to upstyle your footwear as well, whether you're wearing flats or heels.

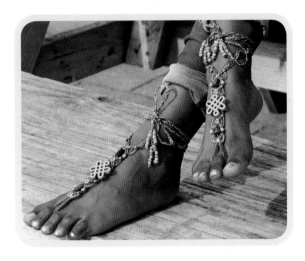

## Adding visual interest

This project uses the berry knot to create the holding section of a plant hanger, but there's no reason it can't be used to add detail to other parts of your project as well. Here Laura Ayres-Selent of the Vintage Loop has used berry knots to add visual interest to the hanging ropes (left). Using them with the plant hanger in this way with the bright red cord helps evoke the idea of Fall berries, or maybe even some summer strawberries? Try adding berry knots into other projects, such as bracelets or anklets, to make them a little more textured and exciting.

# Towel Rack

*by* EMMA RADKE

## Square Knot Sinnet

The up-and-coming designer Emma Radke was taught macramé by her grandmother. It was a stint of unemployment that became the impetus for Radke to experiment with making more than simple jewelry pieces. She began researching contemporary macramé online and was inspired by what she was saw of the reinvention of the craft. A short while later she made her first hammock chair and opened an Etsy store, making and selling commissioned pieces.

### ABOUT THE TOWEL RACK

A truly modern application of all the technical elements of this craft, the towel rail combines cotton cord and bamboo to create a stylish piece for your apartment. Fully portable, you could hang this on a hook in your bathroom and then move it outside to let the towels dry.

### ABOUT THE SQUARE KNOT SINNET

A sinnet is created by repeatedly tying a knot to form a longer, knotted section. In this case, the square knot (see page 44) is used. A sinnet will generally require a minimum of five knots to be classified as such. This technique is popular in plant hangers, bookmarks, bracelets, and much more. Once you have mastered the square knot, the sinnet is an easy, natural progression. If creating a custom piece with specific size requirements, Radke often plots the piece on gridded paper.

## Tip

Radke suggests buying bamboo in a 48-in (122-cm) length. The pole will be naturally tapered, so cut it in half and use the thicker piece at the top. This will allow the towel to drape nicely over the lower bar.

## You will need

- A strong metal ring about 2 in (5 cm) diameter

- Four pieces of $\frac{1}{4}$-in (6-mm) gauge rope 40 ft (12 m) in length

- A swivel or working hook, fixed to something sturdy, so that the cords hang down while you work

- Two pieces of 1–2-in (2.5–5-cm) diameter dowel 24 in (60 cm) in length

- Scissors

## Other knots used

- Lark's head knot, page 18

- Square knot, page 44

- Double half hitch knot, page 72

# How to Tie a Square Knot Sinnet

1: Using a wrap knot or lark's head knot (see pages 18 or 38), attach the midpoints of two working cords 24 in (60 cm) in length to a ring. Take the left cord over the two cords in the center and then under the cord on the right. The cord will make a "C" shape.

2: Take the right cord under the two cords in the center, making a "D" shape, then bring the cord up through the center of the "C," and over the left cord.

3: Bring the cord now on the right back over the center cords and under the cord now on the left.

4: Take the now left cord under the center cords and then up through the "D" and over the right cord.

5: Repeat steps 1–4 at least five times (or more as desired) to make a sinnet.

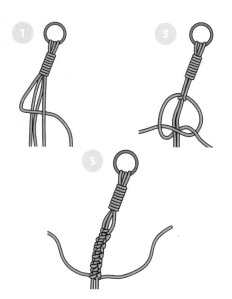

# How to Make the Towel Rack

1: Fold each cord in half and attach the midpoints to the ring with a lark's head knot (see page 18). You will have eight cords of even length hanging from the ring. Group four cords on the left (group A) and four cords on the right (group B).

2: Using the two cords on the left in A as working cords, tie a square knot sinnet 15 in (38 cm) in length (or, approximately 17–18 square knots) around the two remaining cords (inactive cords) in A. Repeat step 2 for the group B cords.

3: To secure the first bamboo rail, use the two inactive cords in A to tie a double half hitch knot (see page 72) around the rail. Repeat with group B to secure the other end of this rail.

4: Holding the A cords as tightly as possible, tie a square knot (see page 44) with the same cords you worked with in step 3. The working cords and inactive cords should now be reversed. Repeat step 4 for the B cords.

5: Continue tying square knots to make an 18-in (46-cm) sinnet in A and B cords.

6: Repeat step 3 to secure the second bamboo rail.

7: Repeat step 4.

8: Finish the towel rack with an overhand knot (see page 9). Trim excess cords and tuft up the cord ends.

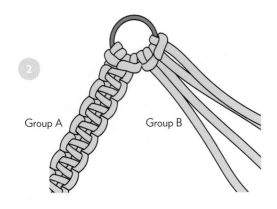

Group A      Group B

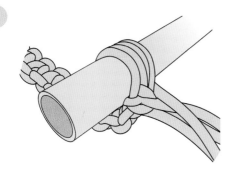

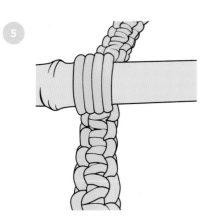

# Another Idea to Try

## Bamboo shelf

One of Radke's handmade pieces, the bamboo shelf (below), highlights the elegant simplicity of this style of sinnet knot. Thinking about the materials that will work best for your project is important. Consider where you want to hang the shelf and what will be on it before you select the rope color and the shelving material.

# Monkey's Fist Ornament

*by* CASSANDRA SMITH

## Monkey's Fist Knot

Designer, Cassandra Smith is known for painting geometric, modern designs onto natural items and traditional forms. Smith says it all started a few years back, with an idea to paint her trademark geometric designs onto a pair of deer antlers. Smith is no stranger to working across mediums, more recently adding macramé—specifically, the monkey's fist knot—into her repertoire.

### ABOUT THE MONKEY'S FIST ORNAMENT

This knot is so interesting, it stands out as an object on its own. Because this knot has nautical origins, it lends itself to designs with the same theme and can often be seen used as party decorations. You could also use it as a paperweight or use ship rope and make this knot into a doorstop.

### ABOUT THE MONKEY'S FIST KNOT

As well as being used as a decorative knot in macramé and other crafts, the monkey's fist knot also has practical applications. This nautical knot was originally used as a weight or anchor at the end of a heavy line. Traditionally, the monkey's fist knot was tied using an individual's palm or extended fingers, or both. Nowadays, designers and crafters use a range of different tools to create the knot. Depending on how often you plan to tie this knot, you might consider using anything from three pencils taped together to a purpose-built tool, purchased from a crafting store.

## You will need

- Three-strand cotton rope, $\frac{3}{8}$-in (10-mm) diameter, 8 ft (2.5 m) in length. This will give the ornament a 10-in (25-cm) drop

- Masking tape

- A $1\frac{1}{2}$-in (4-cm) diameter wooden ball

- Acrylic craft paints

- A variety of differently sized paintbrushes (preferably old ones as the rope can damage the bristles)

## Tip

When it comes to painting your ornament, think about your color palette—decide whether you want to go for contrasting colors, as Smith has, or complementary colors.

# How to Tie a Monkey's Fist Knot

1: In this instance, use the materials for the DIY project (see You Will Need on the previous page) for this knot tutorial. Lie the cord over your open palm—use your non-dominant hand as the holding hand. The short length should be resting behind your hand and the rest of the cord over your palm. Most of the wrapping is done with the longer length of cord so allow for that—the short end need only be long enough to tie off.

2: Wrap the longer length of cord (the working cord) down and over the back of your hand, twice. Wrap across your palm towards the base of your fingers. By the time you are finished you will have three loops of cord lying over your palm, the working cord will be nearest your fingers.

3: Take the working cord and tuck the end behind the three strands of the loops closest to you and pull through from the left side to the right. Then gently remove the cord from your hand, ensuring you maintain the loops you have created.

4: Take the longer length of cord and wrap it horizontally around the three full loops (all six strands), three times. This will encompass all strands in a loose wrap. Don't wrap too tightly as you want these to "hold" the wooden ball. Insert the ball into the center of the monkey's fist knot.

5: Tuck the tip of the working cord and loop it, from bottom to top, behind the horizontal strands created in step 4.

6: Take the working cord and wrap it down and over, encapsulating the ball and the horizontal strands—leave the original loops out of this, wrapping only the horizontal strands. Repeat three times, working from the left of the loops to the right.

7: Working your way along all the loops tied in steps 1–6, gently tug the loops, one by one, to firm up the knot.

8: Find where the working cord comes out of the ornament and tuck the end of the cord firmly and deeply inside the ornament. This becomes the hanging loop for your ornament.

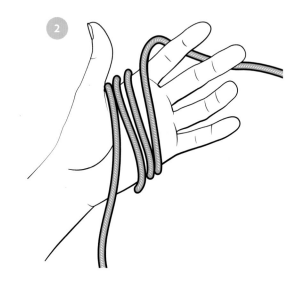

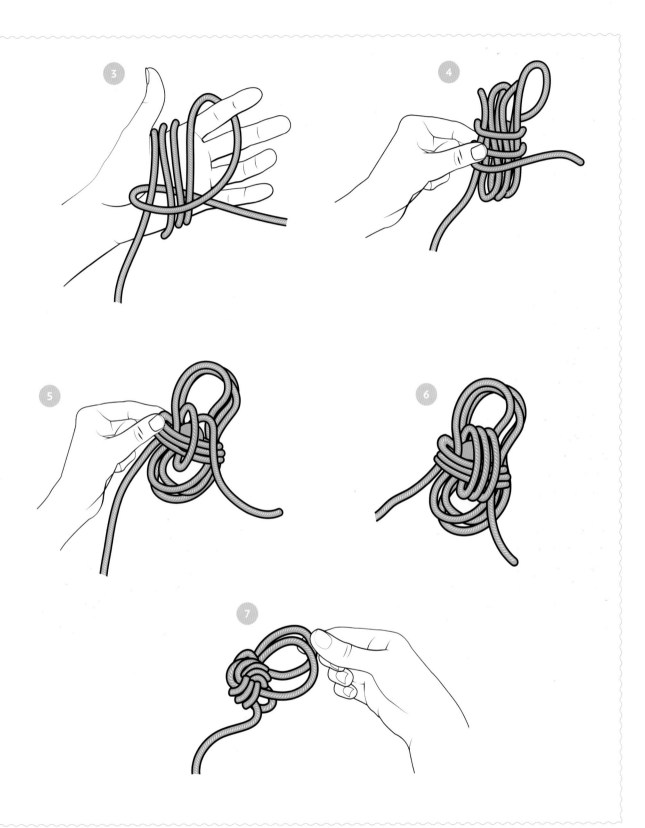

# How to Make the Monkey's Fist Ornament

1: Wrap the ends of the rope in the cream-colored tape to prevent fraying. Repeat steps 1–8 on the previous pages.

2: Once you have finished tying the knot, tuck the ends of the rope into the knot. You will need to be fairly forceful, and may want to use the end of a paintbrush to do so, but once they are in they will stay put.

3: Use a length of masking tape that is long enough to section off a portion of the knot. Try to position the tape so that it cuts across the knot at an interesting angle, and make sure you leave enough room for two other paint sections to fit as well. This section will be the first color of paint you choose.

4: Using a small, square brush with a sharp edge, carefully paint a line next to the painter's tape, but not touching it. Trace along the line created by the tape to get a crisp edge. When you have traced a line all the way around the knot and it's suitably dry, remove the painter's tape.

5: Using the same color paint, fill in the shape you just made. You can use a larger brush for this process because you want to get into all the nooks and crannies created by the rope. After the paint dries, you may see tiny spots that you missed. Once the paint is dry, go back and touch up.

6: Make sure the first paint color is completely dry before starting this step. Use another piece of masking tape to create another interesting shape on the knot. This shape should connect with the first shape you made.

7: Use a small brush to paint sharp corners where the masking tape and the original paint meet. Do this on both sides.

9: Repeat steps 7–8, this time creating a smaller section that can be filled with the third color. Allow to dry.

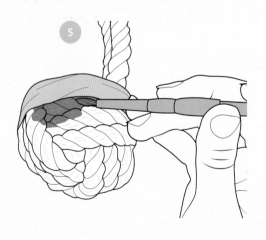

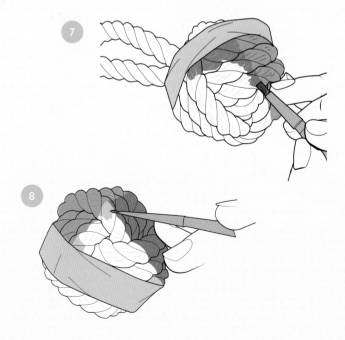

# Other Ideas to Try

## Key ring

This micro-macramé key ring by Mingui Kelly (right) uses waxed polyester thread and a lark's head knot to connect to the key ring. What makes Kelly's work striking is the bold and vibrant colors, here, attractively arranged in stripes across the pad of the key ring; a far cry from traditional monochrome macramé of the past.

## Patterned wall hanging

This wall hanging by Evgenia Garcia (left) is an excellent example of how your macramé skills can be taken to the next level once you master the knots. Garcia used a combination of double half hitches and half hitches as well as a zigzag braid to create this leafy vine pattern. You could create a similar effect with your own patterns using any of the knots shown in this book; good options are the berry knot and square knot in addition to the half hitch and alternating half hitch.

# Petal Earrings

*by* ALESSIA IORIO

## Double Half Hitch Knot

Alessia Iorio, the woman behind Knotted World, is not afraid of experimenting. The self-taught designer has been working with macramé since she was a little girl, learning just enough from a book she bought from a local hobby store to get her started. She is now well known for the precise little pieces—almost miniatures in thread—that she creates and sells on her Etsy store.

### ABOUT THE PETAL EARRINGS ⑤ ⑤

If you've mastered the techniques to make the drop earrings on page 22, this is the perfect next step, showing how a different knot can be applied to jewelry and also showing the exciting effects you can achieve when you use more than one color. The way in which you arrange your threads determines the color patterns that result, so it's worth spending a bit of time planning this in greater detail.

### ABOUT THE DOUBLE HALF HITCH KNOT ⑤ ⑤

The double half hitch knot is one of the main decorative knots used in macramé and features in a wide range of designs and styles. It's simple enough to learn and is a pretty essential knot to master. Remember, practice makes perfect!

## You will need

- Eight pieces of waxed cotton string, in four different colors, 8 in (20 cm) in length. There are 32 pieces of cord in total

- A pair of French hook ear wires with matching rings. The rings must open so they can be attached to the earring wires

- Fabric glue

- Scissors

## Other knot used

- Lark's head knot, page 18

## Tip

Working on such small, precision pieces is best done using a working board. Pin the rings to the board then attach the cords. Make sure you have good, even lighting to work under.

## How to Tie a Double Half Hitch Knot

1: Lay a 5-in (12.5-cm) cord vertically on a working board or tabletop. This is the working cord.

2: Lay a 6-in (15-cm) cord horizontally across the midpoint of the working cord. This is the holding cord. Pin or tape both ends of the holding cord to the working board or tabletop.

3: Take the bottom end of the working cord up and over to the right. Thread it under the holding cord and over the working cord as you pull it back through and down. You have now tightened the first half hitch knot.

4: Move the existing half hitch slightly to the right to make room for the second half of the knot. Repeat step 3, positioning the second half hitch to the right of the first. You have now tied a double half hitch knot.

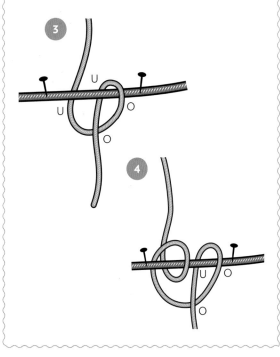

## How to Make the Petal Earrings

1: Attach four cords of the same color (shown here as pink cords) to one of the rings using a lark's head knot (see page 18) to secure each cord. These are the working cords.

2: Attach three cords (inactive cords) in three different colors to the first pair of working cords, using the double half hitch knot instructions on the left.

3: Use your pink working cord to tie a double half hitch knot under the three inactive cord knots.

4: Feed the inactive cords that are nearest the ring (shown here as the yellow cords) over and down in front of the other inactive cords. Knot the left pink cord to the left yellow cord with a double half hitch knot. Repeat for the right pink cord and right yellow cord.

5: Knot the two yellow cords together at the base of the other cords with a double half hitch knot.

6: Make the right inactive cord (now the purple cord) nearest the ring the new working cord. Feed it over the next cord down (here the red cord) and use it to tie a double half hitch knot on the pink and yellow cords on the right. Both the pink and yellow cords act as inactive cords. Repeat this process knotting the purple cord onto the pink and yellow cords on the left.

7: Knot the two purple cords together at the base of the other cords with a double half hitch knot.

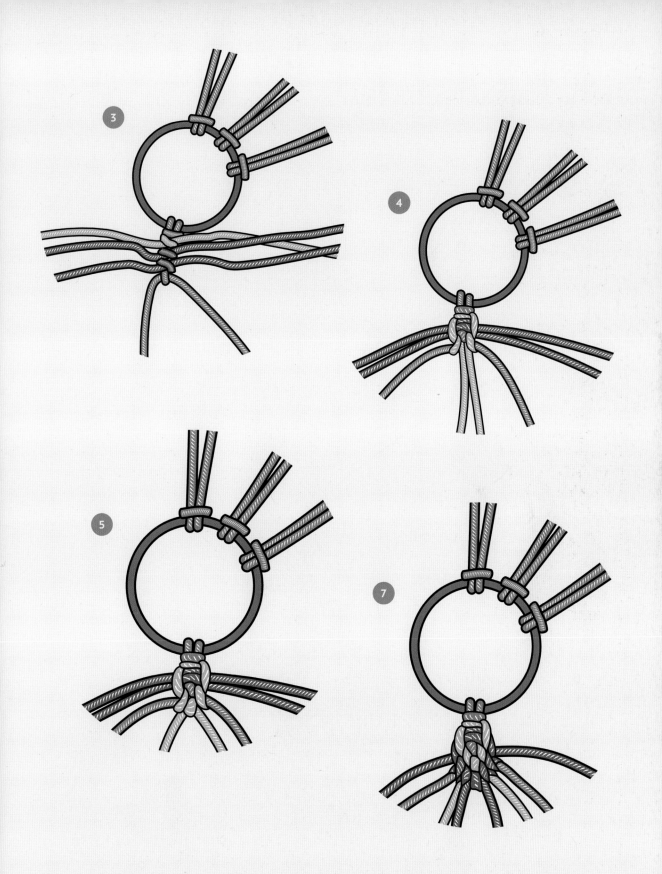

# How to Make the Petal Earrings

8: Repeat step 6 using the red cord on the right as the working cord. Tie double half hitch knots on the pink, yellow, and purple cords on the right. Repeat this process using the red, pink, yellow, and purple cords on the left. You have now formed the first of the four petals for one earring.

9: Repeat steps 2–8 with the three remaining pairs of purple cords to make three more petals.

10: Secure the first and the second petals together by tying a double half hitch knot. Use the pink cord on the right of the first petal as the working cord, and the pink cord on the left of the second petal as the inactive cord.

11: Using the left pink cord from step 10 as a working cord tie double half hitches on the yellow and the purple cords on the left of the first petal. Repeat using the right pink cord and the yellow and purple cords on the right of the second petal.

12: Knot the two yellow cords together at the base of the other cords with a double half hitch knot. One of the yellow cords will be the inactive cord, the other the working.

13: Using the left yellow cord as the working cord and the right purple cord (on the first petal) as the inactive, tie a double half hitch. Repeat using the right yellow cord and the left purple cord on the second petal.

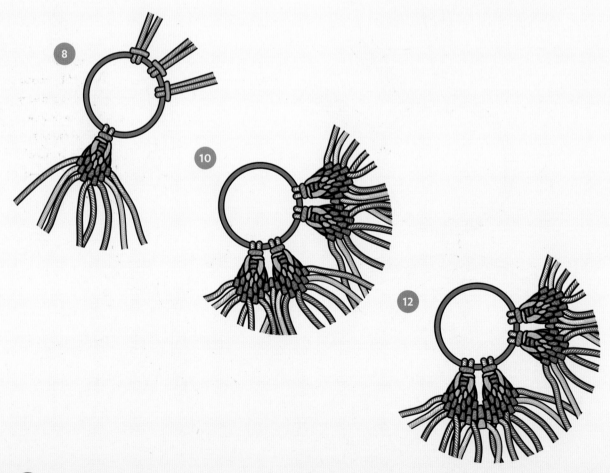

14: Knot the two purple cords together at the base of the other cords with a double half hitch. One of the purple cords will be the inactive cord, the other the working.

15: Repeat steps 10–14 to connect the second petal with the third, and the third with the fourth. When completed, trim excess cord. To make the second earring, repeat steps 1–15.

16: Tuck the edges neatly back on both earring and glue to fix in place.

17: When the glue is dry, open the rings and attach to the earring wires.

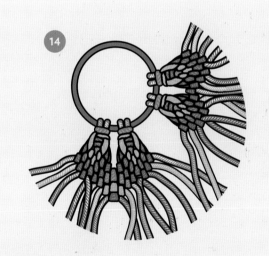

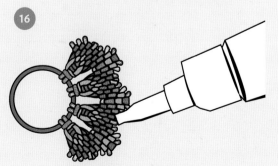

# Another Idea to Try

## Intricate knotting

The double half hitch knot is a great one to use for creating small, intricate pieces. When making this brooch (above), Asmina Fotos of Asmina's Handmade used very fine waxed cord in a soft color to keep the piece delicate and feminine. To add interest, she embellished the tips with beadwork in a contrasting color. If you made two of these, you could fix them to stud findings to make a pair of retro earrings.

# Market Bag

*by* JO ABELLERA

## Horizontal Double Half Hitch Knot

Jo Abellera has been working with macramé, under the moniker of KKIBO, since deciding to expand her brand's focus from knitwear and textiles to include the knot-based craft. "Macramé came into my range after someone asked if I could make hanging baskets," says Abellera. These days Abellera has been known to turn her hand to plant hangers, bags, and wall hangings. She also teaches macramé workshops in her home city of Los Angeles.

### ABOUT THE MARKET BAG ⑤ ⑤ ⑤

Stylish and eco friendly, this market bag is definitely a project you should start once you've practiced your knotting skills and are feeling confident enough to take on a larger scale project. If you want to make a bag that can be used for carrying smaller items, lessen the gaps between the rows of horizontal knots.

### ABOUT THE HORIZONTAL DOUBLE HALF HITCH KNOT ⑤ ⑤

This knot is decorative and diverse. It is often used in pieces like market bags, plant hangers, and belts. Once mastered, it is simple to reproduce but it may require a period of trial and error to perfect, especially if working with different cords or materials. Before making a start on the market bag, take time to practice this knot on a swatch or on a small scale.

### Tip

If you are experimenting with a new design, consider using the finished prototype for a while to put it to the test. "Once I complete something, I will use it every day for weeks or months to evaluate how it works in the real world," recommends Abellera.

## You will need

- Working board, preferably 14 in x 18 in (36 cm x 45 cm)

- Paper, marker pen, and ruler to draw working guide lines

- Forty-four pieces of jute, rope, or another cord of your choice, 9 ft (2.7 m) in length, two pieces 18 ft (5.5 m) in length, and two pieces 11 ft (3.4 m) in length. You can be creative when choosing materials, but Abellera recommends cords no thicker than $1/4$ in (6 mm)

- Sewing pins or T-pins

- Fabric glue

- Scissors

- Fabric dye (optional)

## Other knots used

- Lark's head knot, page 18

- Square knot, page 44

# How to Tie a Horizontal Double Half Hitch Knot

1: Lay a 5-in (12-cm) cords horizontally on a working board—this is the holding cord. To keep it taut pin both ends securely in place.

2: Bring the working cord down behind the holding cord and bring it up and over the holding cord again in a counterclockwise direction. Take the working cord under the holding cord and then over the working cord and pull to secure. This is a half hitch knot.

3: Repeat step 2 to make a line of half hitch knots. Two half hitch knots make a double half hitch knot when tied from left to right.

Note: This knot can also be tied from right to left by bringing up end of the working cord and knotting, as above, but in a clockwise direction.

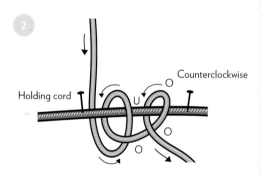

**ALTERNATIVE METHOD**

# How to Make the Market Bag

**Preparing the Working Board**

1: Approximately 2 in (5 cm) from the top of the working board cut two horizontal notches on either side of the board. At the top center of the board, cut one vertical notch. These notches will help secure the holding cord as you work with it.

2: Draw lines connecting the horizontal notches.

3: At 3½-in (9-cm) intervals, draw parallel lines, horizontally, across the board. These lines will help keep the knots organized and evenly spaced.

**Making the Strap for the Market Bag**

1: Find the midpoints of the two 18 ft (5.5 m) cords and the two 11 ft (3.5 m) cords by folding in half. Align all the midpoints and slide the cords into the top center notch. Four cords—two long working cords and two short filler cords—will fall to the front and also to the back of the board. Tie a square knot (see page 44) using the four cords at the front. Tie 29 more square knots.

2: Turn the strap upside down, return to the midpoint, and complete the square knot. Tie 30 more square knots with the remaining cord on the other side and set the strap aside.

**STRAP**

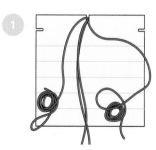

## Making the Front and Back of the Market Bag

1: Take one of the 9-ft (2.7-m) cords and lay it horizontally across the board, securing it in the notches made earlier. This will be the holding cord for the knots that will form the bag's opening.

2: Attach the midpoints of five nine-foot cords to the holding cord with lark's head knots (see page 18). Mentally number these cords, from left to right, 1–10.

3: Tie horizontal double half hitch knots on cord 1 (the holding cord) with cords 2, 3, 4, and 5, in that order.

4: Using cord 10 as a holding cord and working from right to left, make horizontal half hitch knots on cords 9, 8, 7, and 6, in that order.

5: Cross the holding cords (1 and 10) at the center to make an x and pin to secure.

## FRONT AND BACK

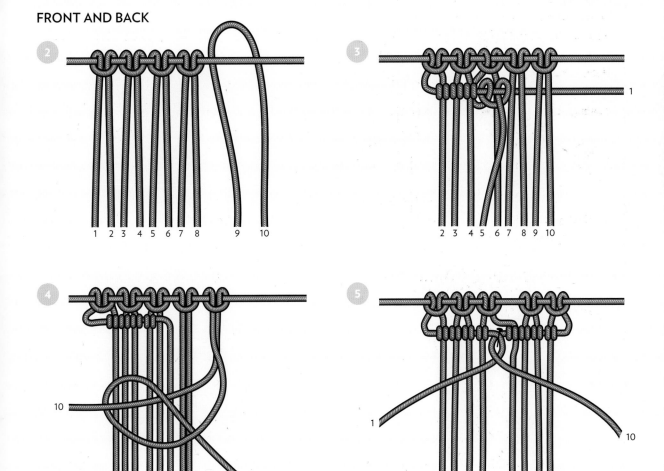

# How to Make the Market Bag

6: Using cord 1 as the holding cord, and working from right to left, tie horizontal half hitch knots on cords 5, 4, 3, and 2. Keep the knots as close to one another as possible while tying.

7: Take cord 10 and make this your new holding cord and working from left to right, tie horizontal double half hitch knots on cords 6, 7, 8, and 9.

8: Pin cord 1 onto the second horizontal line you have drawn on the board.

9: Take cords 6, 7, 8, and 9 and cross them over cords 2, 3, 4, and 5, creating an "X".

10: Using cord 1 as the holding cord, tie horizontal half hitch knots, using cords 6, 7, 8, and 9 along the line drawn on your board.

11: Secure cord 10 onto the board. Tie horizontal double half hitches onto cord 10 with cords 5, 4, 3, and 2.

## FRONT AND BACK

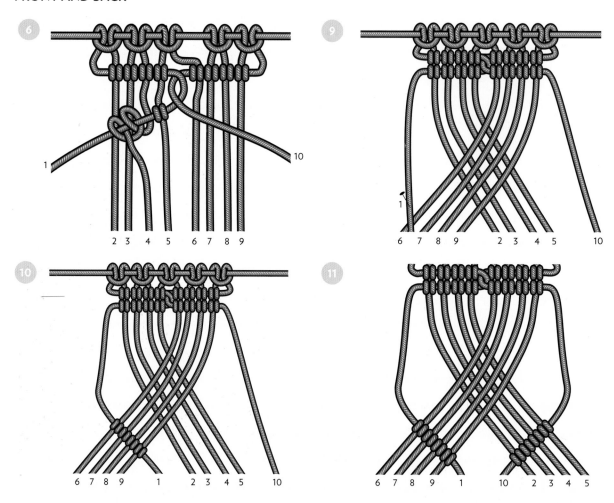

12: Cross cords 1 and 10. Tie horizontal half hitch knots onto cord 1 with cords 9, 8, 7, and 6, in that order.

13: With holding cord number 10, working left to right, tie horizontal half hitches with cords 2, 3, 4, and 5. Continue in this way, working until you have 4 squares of this X pattern.

14: Mount five more lark's head knots to the right of the four squares.

15: Work the first row of horizontal double half hitches, as per the instructions in step 3–7.

16: Before securing the holding cord to complete the first square, twist the cord twice to connect it to the square on the left. Make sure to use as many pins as you need to secure the cord, and also to ensure you are creating squares of equal size. Continue repeating the process from steps 8–13.

17: Continue working until you have 16 squares, all interconnected.

18: Remove your macramé from the board and set aside. Repeat steps 1–17 to make the back of the market bag.

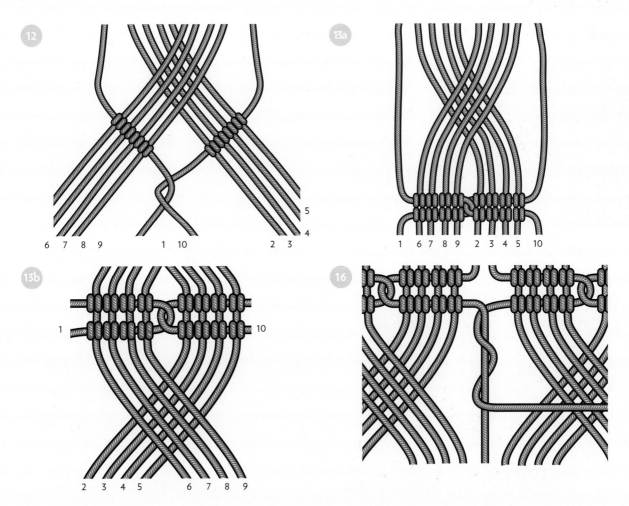

# How to Make the Market Bag

**Making the Side Pieces for the Market Bag**

1: Place the front and back panels of the bag alongside each other on the working board. Overlap the cords at the top—the shorter side of the rectangle, creating the holding cord for the first side of the bag.

2: Using one more 9-ft (2.9-m) cord, find the midpoint by folding it in half. With a lark's head knot, tie it onto the overlapping holding cords. Repeat with one more 9-ft (2.7-m) cord.

3: Position one end of the strap at the top, in between the two lark's head knots. The four cords at the end of the

strap should sit underneath the two overlapping holding cords.

4: Secure the strap to the bag by tying four horizontal half hitch knots.

5: You should now have ten cords. Use the ten cords to tie four more X squares (see steps 6–13, Making the Front and Back of the Market Bag). Note: Make sure to twist the cord on both sides now (to connect the squares of the bag) as you work your way down.

6: Repeat steps 1–5 for other side of the strap.

## SIDES

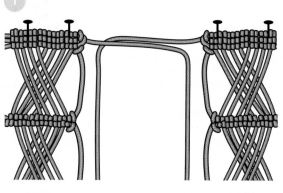

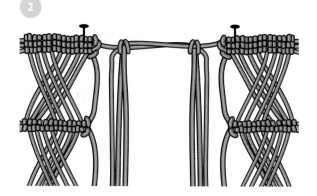

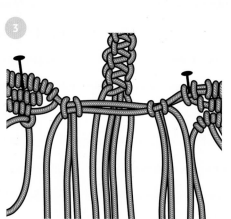

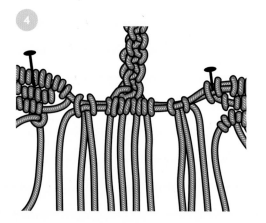

## Making the Bottom Piece for the Market Bag

1: Turn the bag inside out and find the two center cords from each of the side panels you just finished tying. Run these two sets of cords along the bottom of the bag toward each other so they overlap to create the "spine" for the bottom.

2: Starting at one end of the bag, tie a square knot using one strand from the front and one strand from the back of the bag as the working cords and the spine as the inactive, holding cords. Pull the knot tight.

3: Pick up the next two strands (one from the front and one from the back) and tie the next square knot. Continue doing this along the spine until the bottom of the bag is closed.

4: Using fabric glue, place a bead of glue underneath all the square knots. Let the glue dry before cutting off the fringe and turning right side out.

## BOTTOM

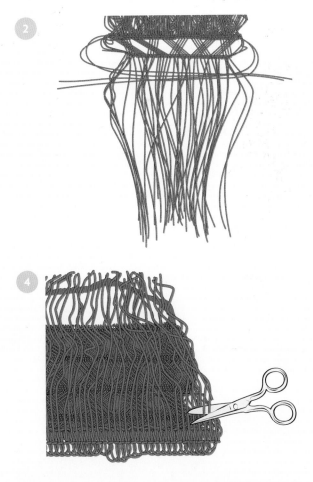

# Other Ideas to Try

## Detachable bag strap

When creating this detachable handbag strap, Erica Maree chose bright, contrasting colors that really attract the eye. If you are planning on making something similar, think about using colors that will either tone or contrast with your collection of bags. If you have a handbag with a bit a detailing in another color, why not pick this out when making your strap? Also think about the material you are going to use—Maree chose hardwearing nylon cord for hers, but you could also use leather, paracord, or strips of canvas.

## Statement jewelry

Statement jewelry pieces are a great project to make with macramé. The contrast between the simple, subtle cord and a semiprecious gemstone can make an item look really unusual and exciting! When creating this beautiful statement necklace (right), Tato Dobien of Amonithe used a large piece of tourmilated quartz to create drama, but paired it with a simple navy waxed thread and pearl beadwork to ensure it remained classic. He also stuck to simple knots, such as the double half hitch knot, to keep it pared back.

# Table Runner

*by* CHARLENE SPITERI

## Diagonal Double Half Hitch Knot

When asked what she likes most about macramé, designer Charlene Spiteri's answer is suitably succinct: "Macramé essentially only requires three basic tools—cord, knot techniques, and imagination." Spiteri's main interest lies in the fact that a simple change can have a significant impact on the resulting work.

### ABOUT THE TABLE RUNNER 🌀🌀

A table runner is a great project to show off this knotting technique. The cord forms a wonderful pattern between the knots, creating an elegant fan-like effect that runs along the table. It's best if you use thick cord as the material acts as a table protector as well

### ABOUT THE DIAGONAL DOUBLE HALF HITCH KNOT 🌀🌀

The real beauty of this knot can be seen in its repetition. For this reason it is in its element when used to create a table runner, wall hanging, or a piece of jewelry. According to Spiteri, this knot is rather flexible in that it can "be designed to look very bold or subtle."

## You will need

- Measuring tape, grid paper, and a pencil

- To make a table runner approximately 53 in x 9 in (135 cm x 23 cm): eight pieces of cord 14 ft (4.3 m) in length, and one piece—the anchor cord—10 ft (3 m) in length. For a table runner of different dimensions, see page 89

- A 10–12-in (25–30-cm) piece of wooden dowel on which to work the macramé. The dowel is removed when the runner is completed

- Sharp scissors

## Other knot used

- Lark's head knot, page 18

## Tip

Macramé can sometimes be a numbers and calculation game, so before you commence a project make sure you have a working knowledge of the techniques and a good understanding of the cord lengths and the materials required. For this project, prepare by experimenting with cords of different colors and thicknesses before commencing.

# How to Tie a Diagonal Double Half Hitch Knot

1: Attach four working cords about 30 in (75 cm) in length to a piece of secured cord or to a piece of dowel with lark's head knots (see page 18).

2: The diagonal double hitch knot can be worked from the right or the left. Here, we have chosen to start on the left. Take the far left cord. Pick it up and lay it diagonally over the other cords. This is the diagonal holding cord onto which you will be tying the knots.

3: Take the next cord on the left—this will be the working cord—bring it underneath the holding cord and loop it up, around, and down. As you pull on the working cord, it should come over the holding cord at

the bottom. Pull the working cord tightly and ever so slightly to the left. Repeat to create a double half hitch.

4: Repeat step 3 with all the working cords, securing each to the diagonal holding cord with a double hitch knot. A raised bar will form along the holding cord if the knots are being tied correctly.

5: When you have tied all the working cords to the holding cord, take the holding cord and run it diagonally over the top of the working cords, from right to left. Repeat steps 2–4, but this time tying the working cords in sequence from right to left.

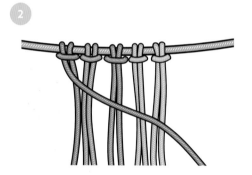

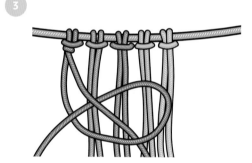

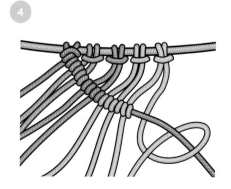

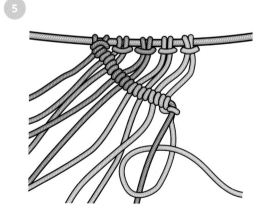

# How to Make the Table Runner

You can vary the length of the table runner by adding more or fewer diagonal double hitch knot rows. You can also make it wider by adding more cords. Measure the length of the table and depending on the angle of the diagonal, you can work our how many diagonal repeats are needed. Follow the schema below and right, using your measurements, by drawing on a 1:4 scale on grid paper.

1: Fold the eight long lengths of cord in half. Tie each of these working cords to the dowel using a lark's head knot (see page 18). Again using a lark's head knot, secure one end of the anchor cord to the dowel to the left of the first working cord, making sure there is 2 in (5 cm) of free cord trailing on the left and the longer length of cord trailing on the right. Start on the right, using the first of the 16 working cords to tie a double half hitch knot to the anchor cord just under the dowel. Continue tying double half hitch knots horizontally along the anchor cord with the remaining 15 cords staying close to the dowel. The anchor cord will now be on the right.

2: Pick up the anchor cord and run it diagonally (from right to left) over the top of the working cords. Measure 6 in (15 cm) from the dowel down the first working cord on the left. Tie the anchor cord to this cord with a hitch knot. This will keep the anchor cord in place while making diagonal hitch knots with each of the working cords.

3: For the runner to be an even width (about 9 in/ 23 cm) along its length, the hitch knots should be touching each other. You can adjust the knots throughout the process if they are not sitting flush. To do this, pull the anchor cord slightly and move the knots closer together.

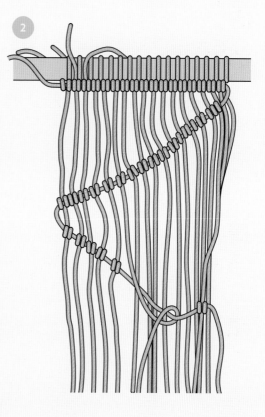

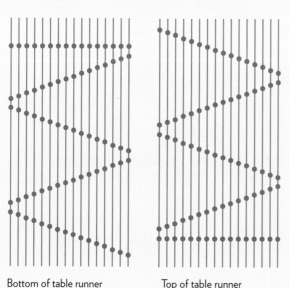

Bottom of table runner        Top of table runner

# How to Make the Table Runner

4: Continue creating rows of diagonal hitch knots in a zigzag pattern until you have completed seven (more or less if you are working to your own measurements) diagonals.

5: Tie the final row of hitch knots horizontally. If these instructions have been followed, you will be tying from left to right. Cut the anchor and working cords 1½ in (4 cm) below the final horizontal row.

6: Slide the runner off the dowel. Cut each working loop dead center to make 1½-in (4-cm) strands. Cut the anchor cord so that it is also 1½ in (4 cm) in length.

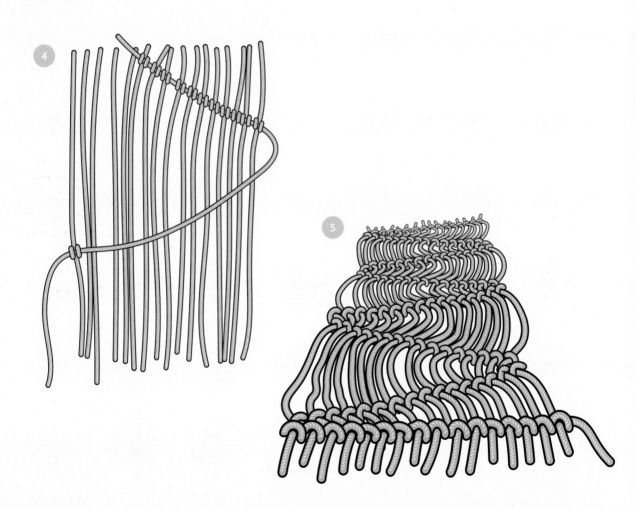

# Other Ideas to Try

## Friendship bracelet

Friendship bracelets are a popular project choice when starting this craft, but why not make yours a little different? Using a hard-wearing braided line with metal findings, as Anastasia Khazybekava of Thread Design Studio did here (right), helps turn your bracelet into a more substantial and long-lasting piece of jewelry, while the use of the diagonal double hitch knot creates a delicate and pretty pattern.

## Master diagonal knots

In this wall hanging by Jo Jansen (left) we can see the creative potential of mastering knots that work on the diagonal. Jansen uses a combination of vertical, horizontal, and diagonal double half hitch, or clove hitch knots, combined with a square knot to make this simple wall hanging more visually exciting. To make your macramé piece even more interesting, why not think about making your piece mixed media by including materials like bamboo or driftwood?

# Chevron Pendant

*by* MEGAN TODD

## Right-Hand and Left-Hand Double Knot

Australian-based designer Megan Todd has been working with rope under the moniker of Knots & Knits for more than four years. The focus of her work is close to home and centers on a desire to support local and small businesses. The idea of bringing traditional handicrafts like macramé to the modern world appeals to her and this is reflected in the work she creates as she uses simple, classic methods to craft items that are current and contemporary.

### ABOUT THE CHEVRON PENDANT

This chevron pendant is a stylish and modern twist on a traditional look. Though the knot takes a little practice, it's unique because it allows you to create a pattern within your design and then the knot gets to be the showpiece. Todd's design here uses four colors, but you could go monochrome or even double the pattern and use eight colors instead.

### ABOUT THE RIGHT-HAND AND LEFT-HAND DOUBLE KNOT

Like many of the macramé knots featured in the second half of the book, this project involves an intricate technique that may take a couple of attempts to master. It is worth sticking with it, as once you get the hang of the technique it will prove very versatile. The right-hand and left-hand double knot can be used to create something familiar, like a friendship bracelet, or something altogether different like a living room rug.

## You will need

- Six pieces of $^3/_{16}$-in (5-mm) cord, rope, or jute 5 ft (1.5 m) in length in a mixture of colors and textures

- Jewelry chain or a length of leather thong from which to hang the macramé pendant

- Working board

- Masking tape

- Scissors

- Disposable lighter to cut and seal cord ends (not required if using jute or yarn)

## Other knot used

- Lark's head knot, page 18

## Tip

If you are working with yarn made up of more than one thread, pay particular attention to loose threads. "Ensuring that the work is all neat and tucked in nicely is the key," recommends Todd.

# How to Tie a Right-Hand and Left-Hand Double Knot

## Right-Hand Knot

1: To make the right-hand double knot, begin with two cords 12 in (30 cm) in length. Take the left cord over the right cord to form a shape that resembles the number 4.

2: Take the left cord under the right cord and then up over the left cord.

3: Push the right cord up the holding cord (keeping this taut) until the knot is tight, Repeat step 1–3 using the same cord, to make a right-hand double knot.

Right-hand knot

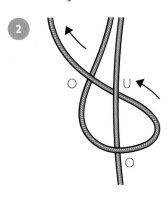

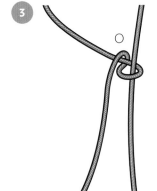

## Left-Hand Knot

1: To make the left-hand double knot, start with two cords fixed to a working board. Take the right cord over the left cord to form a shape that resembles the number 4 in reverse.

2: Take the right cord under the left cord and then up over the right cord.

3: Push the left cord up the holding cord (keeping this taut) until the knot is tight. Repeat steps 1–3 using the same cord, to make a left-hand double knot.

Left-hand knot

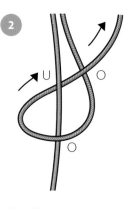

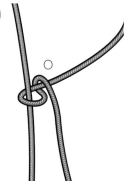

# How to Make the Chevron Pendant

1: Gather the six cords together and secure the chain or leather thong around their midpoint using a lark's head knot (see page 18).

2: Secure the chain or thong and the cords to the working board with masking tape, as shown. Using the top two cords to the left of the chain, tie a right-hand double knot. (Remember to tie two knots on the cord!) Tie four more right-hand double knots.

3: Using the top two cords to the right of the chain, tie a left hand double knot. Tie three more left-hand double knots. The left-hand and right-hand double knots should come together at the base of the cords. Knot the right and left cords together using a left-hand double knot.

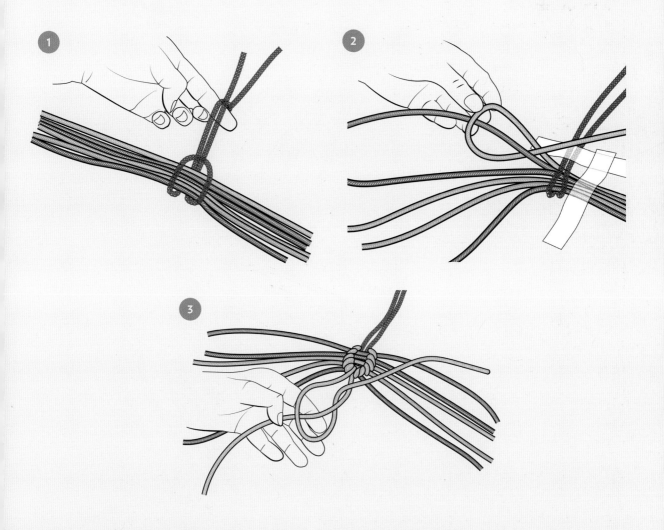

# How to Make the Chevron Pendant

4: Repeat steps 2–4 using the topmost cord and the cord below on the left, and then the topmost cord and the cord below on the right. Do not forget to tie a right hand double knot to join left and right together.

5: Repeat steps 2–4 with the next uppermost pairs of cords to the left and to the right. Keep repeating until you have six chevrons of double knots. Trim cord ends to your preferred length and seal using a lighter if necessary.

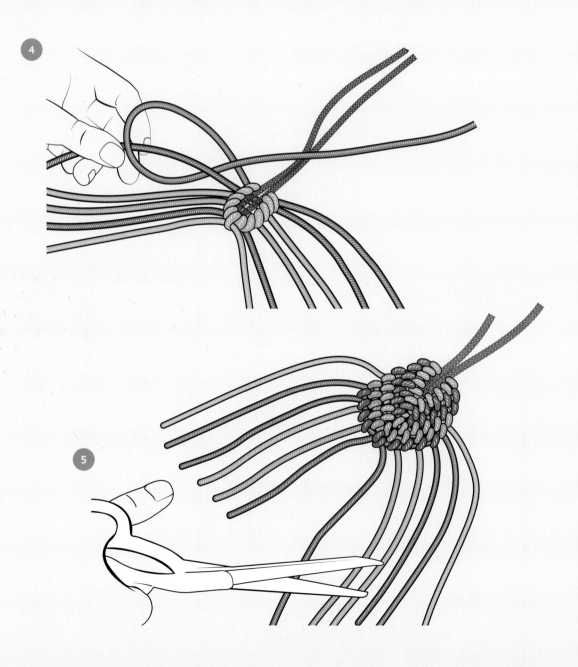

# Other Ideas to Try

## Tank top straps

Laura Pifer's blog features a plethora of items that show macramé innovatively applied to clothes and here she's cleverly refashioned a decorative strap for a tank top (right). Items like this are a great way to upcycle clothes and you could achieve something similar by cutting up an old T-shirt into strips that can be knotted into straps. See page 115 for a tutorial to make something similar.

## Crystal necklaces

MacK Mars creates delicate pieces of jewelry with natural crystals. He felt that macramé would be the perfect technique to show these stones off in their natural beauty. The simple overhand knots on fine leather strands and embroidery floss creates a delicate shell that holds the crystal as the centerpiece (left). If you look closely, you'll see that the result is similar to a plant hanger, with the difference that you enclose the crystal completely within the knots.

# Cord Bracelet

## Turk's Head Knot

Like many of her contemporaries, Tanya Aguiñiga enjoys the freedom that comes from working with macramé, often combining or inventing new techniques as she goes. Her desire to create unique designs means she tends to avoid over-planning pieces before commencing or restricting her work to a particular technique.

### ABOUT THE CORD BRACELET ⑤

This project is all about showing the knot to full effect and Aguiñiga uses thick cord so that the details of the knot can be seen clearly. Some cord comes pre-dyed, but to recreate what Aguiñiga has done here, simply dip dye the cords once the knot is complete. Another option would be to dye just a few of the strands or paint over the cords once completed.

### ABOUT THE TURK'S HEAD KNOT ⑤ ⑤ ⑤

The beauty of the Turk's head knot is that it is not only suited to making smaller pieces like Aguiñiga's cord bracelet, but it can also be increased in scale to make stools, flat mats, cushions, boxes, lampshades, and—as Aguiñiga points out—"anything else structural."

Once she has established the direction in which she wants the work to go, Aguiñiga starts with small tests that lead on to sketches and then a full-scale piece. She identifies that one of the pitfalls of the Turk's head knot is that the knot has to function perfectly for the final result to work.

### You will need

- An unwanted, cylindrical plastic bottle—soda water bottles work well—with a diameter that will allow the bracelet to slide over the hand. Pins will be pushed into the container.

- Sufficient cord, rope, or yarn to wrap 13 times around the bottle. If you plan to dye the bracelet, chose a plain cord. If not, there is plenty of leeway to use colored or textured cord.

- Masking tape

- Sewing pins or T-pins

- Fabric glue

- Fabric dye (optional)

### Tip

Sewing pins or T-pins are especially useful when first attempting this knot. Between steps, secure the cord by pinning it to the bottle to hold it in place.

# How to Tie the Turk's Head Knot

1: In this instance, please use the materials for the project (see You Will Need on the previous page) for this tutorial. Place the cord over the bottle with 3–4 in (8–10 cm) of cord trailing to the front (the side nearest you). The longer section of cord trails behind the bottle. Wrap the cord around the bottle twice, working to the right. The long cord (the leading cord) will be trailing to the right and to the front of the bottle. The end of the leading cord may fray during the threading, so wrap the end in tape. Pin cords to the bottle.

2: Take the strand on the far left and bring it over the middle strand (first cord to its right) making a "D" shape. Re-pin cord to bottle as shown in step 2.

3: Hold the leading cord and slip it over the first strand to its right, through the center of the "D" and

under the second strand. Pull the leading cord through. The leading cord will now be on the left.

4: As you work the cords around the bottle, roll the bottle a little way toward you each time. Thread the leading cord over the first strand on the far left and under the second strand. Pull the leading cord through to the right.

5: Take the left strand on the bottle and lay it over the strand to its right, making a figure 8 shape. Pin cords to the bottle.

6: Hold the leading cord and slip it over the first strand to its left and under the second strand.

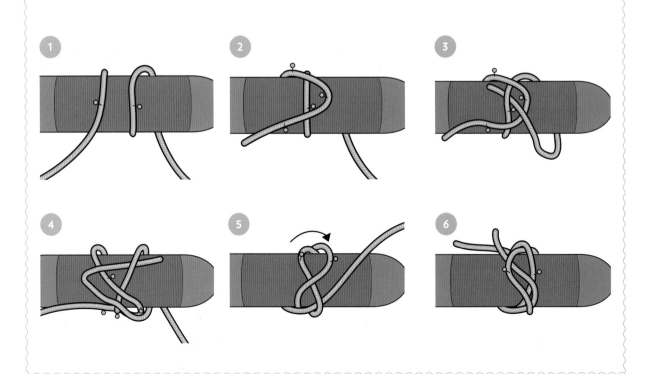

7: At this point, the leading cord will meet the short length of cord. Pull the short end of the cord to the left and begin to follow its path with the leading cord.

8: Take the leading cord and thread it over the first strand on the right (alongside the short end of cord) and under the second. Pull the cord through.

9: Continue threading the leading cord right and left following the path of your previous cord in the same way untill all the gaps between the strands are filled. Each loop on the bracelet should be three-strands wide when it is complete.

10: Remove the pins and slide the bracelet off the bottle.

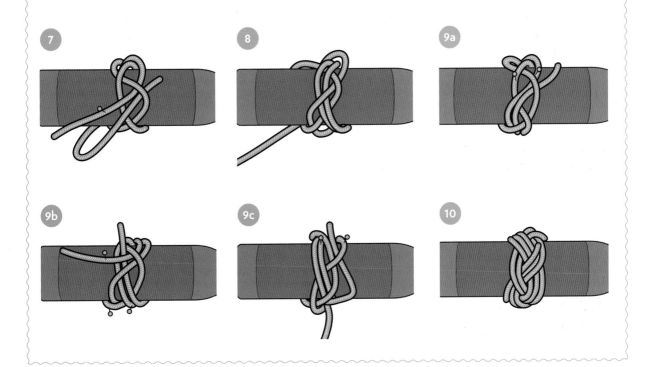

## How to Make the Turk's Head Bracelet

Follow steps 1–10 on these pages. If you want the bracelet to consist of more strands, increase the length of your cord proportionately. Remove your bracelet from the bottle. Trim excess material and conceal and secure cord ends with glue.

Optional: When the glue is dry, make up the dye mixture following package directions. Dip one half of the bracelet into the dye. Hang the bracelet to drip into a tray. When dry, dip again to strengthen the color if necessary.

Grand Hôtel
de Londres

Avenue de Keyser, 58, Anvers

Adresse télégraphique : LONHOTEL - ANVERS
Téléphone no 259/60 (4 lignes)

# Hanging Garland

*by* EMMA RADKE

## Alternating Square Knot

Emma Radke is not one to shy away from a challenge, a fact that can be seen in the scale of some of the custom pieces she makes for clients of her Etsy store, The Throwbackdaze. "I focus mostly on large-scale macramé pieces," Radke reveals. "Swings, shelves, hammock chairs, and others." Recently she has expanded her repertoire to include wall hangings and mixed-media jewelry pieces.

### ABOUT THE HANGING GARLAND

Pieces like this are a lovely and creative way to hang up your photos and pieces of memorabilia. For special occasions these add an extra special touch to homemade bunting and can also be used to create decorative canopies for parties.

### ABOUT THE ALTERNATING SQUARE KNOT

Before attempting the alternating square knot, you will need to have mastered the square knot (see page 44). The technique employed here for the alternating square knot requires four or eight cords—two core strands and two active in each of the groupings. Using different techniques can help you create different patterns and shapes that will breathe new life into the square knot. This technique can be used in macramé bag straps and jewelry or to fill space beautifully in a wall hanging.

## You will need

- A proficiency in the square knot (see page 44)

- To make a garland 10 ft (3 m) long: two pieces of thick jewelry-weight cord 40 ft (12 m) in length. Hemp, jute, or cotton cord will all work. The length of the finished piece will depend on the thickness of the cord, as well as how far apart you space the knots. Thinner cord often goes further than bulkier cord

- A secured dowel or ring to make working the macramé easier

- Scissors

## Tip

When you are familiar with a knotting technique, try to be more strategic about how much cord you will actually need for the project. Over-cutting will lead to unnecessary waste of materials and money.

## Other knots used

- Overhand knot, page 9

- Square knot, page 44

# How to Tie an Eight-Cord Alternating Square Knot

1: Pin eight cords 24 in (60 cm) in length to a working board. The four cords on the left are group A; the four on the right are group B. Using the A, tie a square knot (see page 44) with the outer left and outer right cords as the working cords, and the middle cords as the filler cords. Repeat this knot on group B cords.

2: Select the middle right and outer right cords from A, and the middle left and outer left cords from B. Use these four cords to tie a square knot. The working cords will be the middle right cord from A and the middle left cord from B.

3: Repeat steps 1–2, using the outer left and outer right from the new group A (for the knot shown on the left below), and the outer left and outer right from the new group B (for the knot shown on the right below). Continue with the repetitions several times.

# How to Make the Hanging Garland Using a Four-Cord Alternating Square Knot

For a garland of a different length: multiply the length you want by four.

1: Fold the cords in half. Tie an overhand knot (see page 9) at the midpoint, keeping an open loop at the end that is large enough to pass over a nail or hook. You now have four cords. Hook the loop to the secured dowel or ring. You are now ready to start.

2: Tie a square knot with the outer left and outer right cords. Bring these cords over the inner cords, making them the center cords. Use the new outer left and right cords to tie a square knot, leaving a $\frac{1}{2}$–$1\frac{1}{2}$-in (1.2–4-cm) space between the first and second knots.

3: Repeat step 3 until there is only 7 in (18 cm) of free cord remaining. Double the ends and tie an overhand knot, making sure there is an open loop at the end.

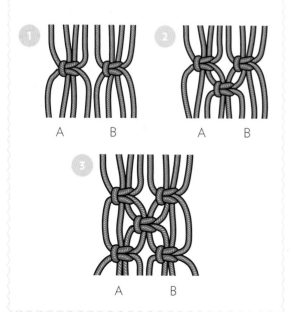

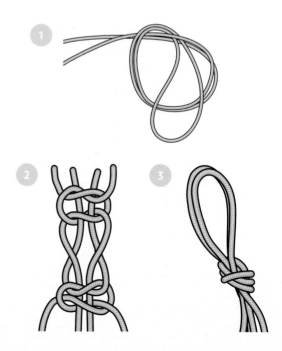

# Other Ideas to Try

## Wall hanging

The alternating square knot does not have to be on small-scale projects. It is such a beautiful knot that it is perfect for creating something larger, such as a statement wall hanging. When creating her contemporary hangings (right), Laura Ayres-Selent of the Vintage Loop uses bright, vibrant colors to make them really stand out. When using this knot to create a hanging, the most important thing is to concentrate on making your knots and the spacing between them even, as that is what creates the beautiful pattern.

## Fringe appeal

Although often used for jewelry, macramé is also a great way of adding detail to clothing. Here, Claudia Rosillo of Texturable used the alternating square knot to customize a bright tee (left). After cutting the bottom of the tee into narrow strips, she then tied several layers of alternating square knots, leaving about 6 in (15 cm) at the bottom to create the fringe. Keeping the macramé design quite simple means this top is very versatile and would look great paired with jeans, dressed up with a simple skirt, or thrown on as a beach coverup.

# Bag Strap

*by* COURTNEY KENNEDY

## Chinese Crown Knot

Courtney Kennedy is the voice behind popular blog Always Rooney. She became interested in macramé when she found a vintage craft book in a thrift store. She got familiar with a few basic knots and then began her first proper project: A macramé bag. After that she began to realize just how versatile the craft was and featured it more and more in her projects. "I love that the possibilities are endless and macramé knots are so versatile," she says.

### ABOUT THE BAG STRAP ⑤ ⑤

This bag strap can also be applied to a range of other items such as a camera strap, a guitar strap, or even straps on a tanktop. As this particular project needs to be strong enough to carry some weight, use hardwearing twine or cord.

### ABOUT THE CHINESE CROWN KNOT ⑤ ⑤ ⑤

The Chinese crown knot is a simple, decorative knot that can add interest to almost any project, from bracelets to keychains. Here it is used in combination with other knots to make a stylish set of loops that connect the flat part of the bag strap to the bag.

## You will need

- Nine pieces of cord 9 ft (3 m) in length
- Working board
- Sewing pins or T-pins
- Two rectangles of leather about 1 in x 3 in (2.5 cm x 7 cm)
- Sewing needle and strong sewing thread
- Scissors

## Other knot used

- Diagonal double half hitch knot, page 88

## Tip

When making the strap using two bunches of multiple cords, tape the ends of each bunch together at the bottom to make it easier to pull the gathered cords through the loops.

# How to Tie a Chinese Crown Knot

1: Fold a piece of cord 36 in (90 cm) in length in half. Secure the midpoint to a working board with a pin. Bring the cord on the left (the working cord) over the cord to its right (the holding cord) and then under the holding cord.

2: Thread the end of holding cord up through the top loop and left over the working cord.

3: Bring the holding cord down over the working cord.

4: Pull the working cord over the holding cord to the left and pull through the loop made by the holding cord on the far right.

5: Pull your knot tightly and adjust to make it even.

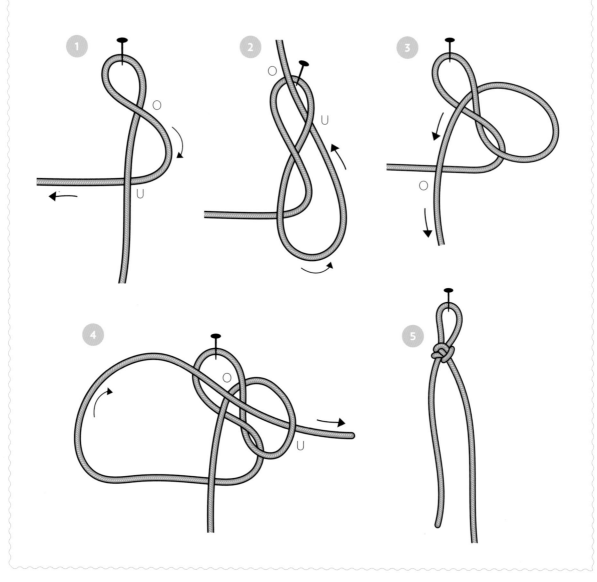

# How to Make the Bag Strap

1: Secure the nine cords close together to the working board with pins. Gather five cords to the left and four cords to the right. Tie a Chinese crown knot with the two groups of cords about 1 in (2.5 cm) down from the pins. Tie six more Chinese crown knots, leaving 1 in (2.5 cm) between each knot.

2: Tie a diagonal double half hitch knot (see page 88) using the cord on the extreme left as the anchor cord, and the other eight cords as working cords.

3: When you have done seven zigzags of diagonal double half hitch knots and the strap is 14 in (35 cm) in length, divide the cords as before—five to the left and four to the right.

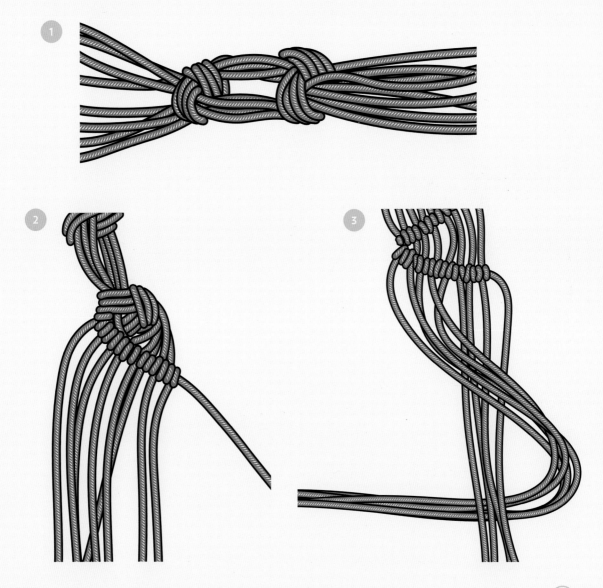

# How to Make the Bag Strap

4: Tie six Chinese crown knots, leaving 1 in (2.5 cm) between each knot.

5: Fold one of the rectangles of leather over the last Chinese crown knot. Stitch ends together.

6: Stitch the leather tag to one side end of the bag. Repeat steps 4-5 for the other end of the strap.

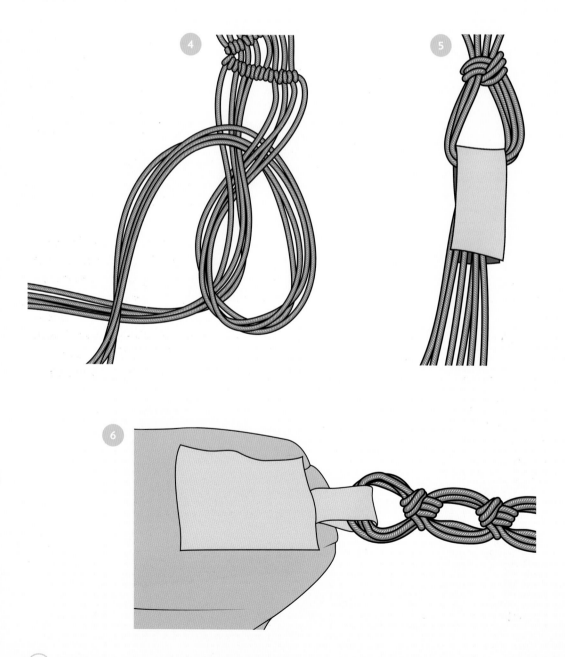

# Other Ideas to Try

## Headphone wire covers

An ideal fusion of tech and craft, Jesika Johnson's headphone covers (right) are a unique twist on boring plastic headphones. She has used a simple repeated half knot to create the pleasing spiral effect, which is offset by the alternating colors. The macramé adds a lovely tactile element to the cords as well as protecting the wire from splitting.

## Plant hanger variation

Sally England has used an attractive series of Chinese Crown knots for decoration and to strengthen the top of her plant hanger (left), preventing it from spinning and twisting on itself. The white pot, rawhide leather, and cotton cord are all fairly plain materials, but the addition of the macramé knots at the top adds a high-end finish to this classic hanging planter. The neutral color scheme would look particularly good with a vividly colored plant.

# Knotted Tank Top

*by* TINO JOHNSON

## Josephine Knot

Tino Johnson stumbled into the world of macramé quite by accident. She wanted to create a sturdy support for a hanging basket in her garden and a friend volunteered to teach her some essential knotting techniques. Pretty soon, she was hooked and now creates a number of macramé items that she sells at local festivals and craft fairs. Johnson likes to experiment with the materials she uses and shies away from always using traditional cord, instead opting to create strands out of recycled materials.

### ABOUT THE KNOTTED TANK TOP

As with Laura Pifer's items shown earlier in the book, these straps are a great way to upcycle your clothes. For this project Johnson decided that the bright pink of the straps added strong visual interest to what is otherwise a plain, black tank top.

### ABOUT THE JOSEPHINE KNOT

The Josephine knot is such a pretty knot that lends itself to a number of applications. Using more than one color shows the knot off in greater detail. A monochrome approach takes away some of the detail in the knot but allows you to create a more textured look. You can also consider bunching the knots closer together for a tight band.

## You will need

- A tank top
- An old T-shirt in a contrasting color, you will cut strips from this to create your contrasting straps
- Scissors
- Sewing pins
- Needle and thread

## Other knot used

- Overhand knot, page 9

## Tip

The Josephine knot can be a bit tricky because you need to tighten the knot slowly as you go. Simply pulling it taut will not create the effect you want, instead, slide it up along the cord until you have the right height and then slowly pull each element of the knot to tighten it evenly.

# How to Tie a Josephine Knot

1: Cut two pieces of cord 25 in (63.5 cm) in length each. Fold the cords in half and tie together using a basic overhand knot (see page 9). Secure to the working board by pinning the top of the loop to the board. Group the four cords into two pairs of working cords.

2: Loop the pair of working cords on the left under the other cords and under itself to make a circle.

3: Take the ends of the pair of working cords on the right and thread them under the trailing ends of

other cords. Forming a loop, take the right working cords over the other cords and then under the cords at the top of the first circle, over itself, and then under the cords at the bottom of the first circle. A second circle has been formed to make a figure eight.

4: Pull gently on the cords to tighten, adjusting as you go to ensure that the knot is even. If you want to keep practicing, repeat steps 1–4 a few inches down from the first knot.

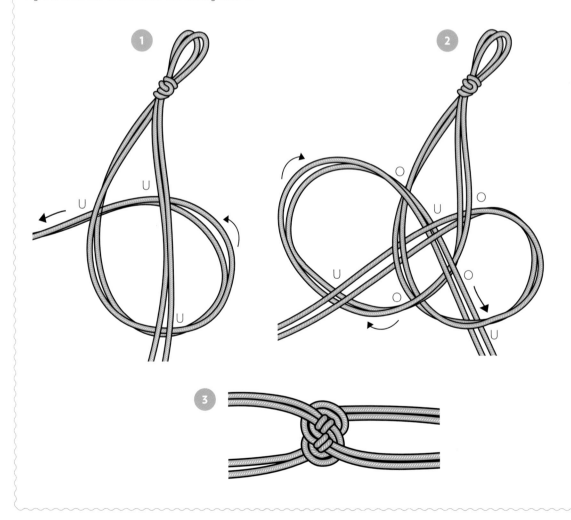

# How to Make the Knotted Tank Top

1: Cut the existing straps off the tank top at the point where they join the top. This tutorial uses a top with very slim straps but if you want to try the project on a vest top, cut the straps slightly lower and hem the cut edge.

2: Then, using a T-shirt in a contrasting color, cut about eight horizontal strips measuring $\frac{1}{2}$ in (12 mm) wide and about 13 in (33 cm) long. Knot two strips together at the top using the overhand knot.

3: Knot about 4 or 5 Josephine knots at $\frac{1}{2}$-in (1-cm) intervals along the cords and repeat this on the other six cords until you have four straps. Untie the overhand knot at the top of each strap.

4: Take two of the cords and join them together with pins so that there is approximately $\frac{1}{2}$ in (1 cm) space between the first knots of the two straps.

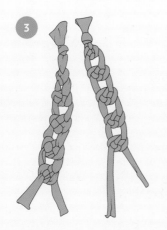

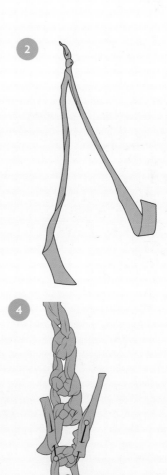

# How to Make the Knotted Tank Top

5: Using matching thread, sew in a few very tiny tacks to secure the two pieces together. Then sew a few hidden stitches (where the stitch is visible on the underside of the strap but doesn't come through to the top of the strap).

6: You should now have a strap that is twice the length. Now pin the two strands of each cord to the front and back of the tank top. Keep the strands separate and pin them about ½ in (1 cm) apart.

7: Use thread that matches the color of the tank top now and again, sew very tiny tacks to secure the strap to the tank top, finishing with a back stitch.

8: Repeat steps 4–7 for the second strap and your tank top is ready to wear.

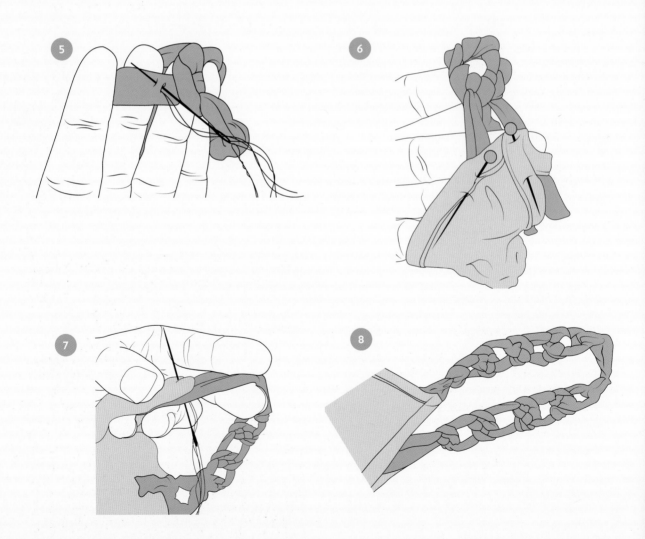

# Other Ideas to Try

## Jade necklace

Originally from Panama, Mingui Kelly travels all around Central America to source unique and beautiful stones for his jewelry, such as turquoise, obsidian, agate, and quartz. This necklace (left) is made from durable waxed polyester thread, which is an ideal material for his fine micro macramé work. The striking jade stone at the center makes this a real statement piece, and the contrast of the smooth stone and textured macramé knotting works perfectly.

## Curtain tie

The Josephine knot can be used in several innovative ways. Because it is decorative enough to stand alone, you can keep it quite loose, allowing gaps to form between. For the curtain tie (right), Tino Johnson bought two bathrobe cords from her local fabric store and placed Josephine knots at 2 in (5 cm) intervals.

# Resources

# Resources

## FURTHER READING

**75 Chinese Celtic & Ornamental Knots: A Directory of Knots and Knotting Techniques Plus Exquisite Jewelry Projects to Make and Wear**
by Laura Williams and Elise Man
(St. Martin's Griffin, 2011)

**The Arts of the Sailor: Knotting, Splicing and Ropework**
by Hervey Garrett Smith
(Dover Publications, 2012)

**Beaded Macramé Jewelry: Stylish Designs, Exciting New Materials**
by Sherri Haab (Potter Craft, 2006)

**Chinese, Celtic & Ornamental Knots for Beaded Jewelry**
by Suzen Millodot (Search Press, 2012)

**Complete Book of Decorative Knots**
by Geoffrey Budworth (Globe Pequot Press, 1998)

**Decorative Fusion Knots: A Step-by-Step Illustrated Guide to New and Unusual Ornamental Knots**
by J.D, Lenzen and Barry Mault
(Green Candy Press, 2011)

**The Knotting & Braiding Bible: The Complete Guide to Creative Knotting Including Kumihimo, Macramé and Plaiting**
by Dororthy Wood (David & Charles, 2014)

**Macramé Pattern Book: Includes Over 70 Knots and Small Repeat Patterns Plus Project**
by Macmillan Publishers
(Macmillan Publishers, 2013)

**Micro Macramé Basics & Beyond: Knotted Jewelry with Beads**
by Raquel Cruz (Kalmbuch, 2014)

**Micro-Macramé: 30 Beaded Designs for Jewelry Using Crystals and Cords**
by Annika deGroot (St. Martin's Griffin, 2009)

**Mod Knots: Creating Jewelry and Accessories with Macramé**
by Cathi Milligan (North Light Books, 2009)

**The New Macramé: Contemporary Knotted Jewelry and Accessories**
by Katie DuMont (Lark Crafts, 2001)

## WEBSITES

**Etsy.com:** From DIY inspiration and downloadable PDF templates to macramé supplies, Etsy really does have it all. This online marketplace is also a great place to window-shop designers or to purchase one-of-a-kind macramé pieces if you're not in the mood to DIY.

**free-macrame-patterns.com:** Once you have mastered all the knots in this book, expand your repertoire with some of the straightforward tutorials that can be found on this site. You will also find a range of macramé patterns and some great projects for kids.

**Instagram.com:** This is another great online source of macramé inspiration. A simple search of #macramé will reveal fantastic works by hobbyists and professional designers from around the globe.

**ouchflower.blogspot.com.au:** This is an Australian-based blog about all things macramé and design. It is well worth your time to check out the knot school and all the posts that are tagged "macramé."

**Pinterest.com:** This is a great source of visual inspiration. It allows you to follow your favorite designer and to keep up with his or her work, or to set up a mood board before starting your next DIY project.

## SUPPLIERS

**beadaholique.com:** A supplier not only offering a range of beads and jewelry fittings, but also macramé cords, working boards, and vintage items.

**cc-craft.co.uk:** Suppliers of cords, tools, and other macramé supplies.

**hobbylobby.com:** Crafting suppliers that offer a good range of macramé must-haves. Hobby Lobby has online shopping.

**kingskountry.com:** A long-established macramé wholesaler.

**macramesuperstore.com:** This company can supply everything you need for a lifetime of macramé.

**spellboundbead.co.uk:** A great source of beads, jewelry findings, and threads aplenty.

**texere-yarns.co.uk:** This is a supplier of a wide variety of yarns and cotton cords.

# Glossary

**Active cord:** Also called the working or leading cord, this is the cord that you are using to create your knots.

**Adjacent:** Cords or knots sitting or positioned next to one another.

**Alternating:** Tying a knot with one cord, and then changing to another cord to tie the next knot.

**Alternating square knots (ASK):** These create a net pattern that is seen in many macramé designs.

**Bar:** A series of knots creating a raised area–horizontal, vertical, or diagonal–in a design.

**Bight:** A folded section of cord.

**Body:** The main part of a macramé item.

**C step:** Part of the process of tying the half knot. The far left cord is placed over the center cords and under the far right cord that will eventually make the "D" shape, thus making a "C" shape.

**Center:** To center cords is to find the midpoint by aligning the ends and folding.

**Cord:** A generic term that describes material that is used to create macramé pieces.

**Diameter:** The width across the center of a strand of cord, a loop, a dowel, bead, or metal ring.

**Double half hitch knot (DHH):** This is two half hitch knots resting side-by-side.

**D step:** Part of the process tying the half knot. The far right cord is placed under the center cords and through the center of the "C," making a "D" shape (see also: C step

**Filler cords:** These are cords, often two or four in number, that run through the center of some knots, like the square knot.

**Fringe:** The ends of cords that have been left to dangle, unknotted.

**Hitch knot:** A knot that is used to attach one or more cords to a dowel, a ring, or another piece of cord.

**Holding cord:** A cord to which knots are tied.

**Inactive cord:** Also called holding or anchor cords, these are the cords that the active cords are knotting around to create your macramé.

**Lark's head knot (LH):** This knot is used to attach one or more cords to a dowel, a ring, or another piece of cord.

**Loop:** A circle or oval made by crossing two parts of a cord.

**Micro-macramé:** Macramé that uses very fine thread to create small knots on smaller pieces such as jewelry.

**Mount:** This is attaching one or more cords to a ring, a handle, a frame, or to another cord.

**Netting:** A pattern of knots, often with a space between knots and rows, created to resemble a net.

**Picot:** These are decorative loops that run along the edges of a macramé design.

**Sinnet (or sennit) knot:** A chain of knots, tied one after the other.

**Spiral knot:** A chain of knots that twists when tied.

**Square knot (SK):** One of the most frequently used knots in macramé.

**Waxed thread:** Cotton or polyester cord coated in a thin coat of wax. The wax coating makes it tougher and helps it to hold its shape better making it perfect for macramé projects.

**Working board:** This can be made from foam, cork, or another material. It is used to secure cords, keeping them taut and/or easily manipulated, while a project is being worked.

**Working cord:** The active cord used to tie a knot.

## ABBREVIATIONS

**O:** Indicates when the working cord goes over the holding cord or any filler cords

**U:** Indicates when the working cord goes under the holding cord or any filler cords

# Contributor Index

## PROJECT CONTRIBUTORS

Alessia Iorio (page 70)
Knotted World, Capua, Italy
www.knottedworld.etsy.com

Cassandra Smith (page 64)
Made By Cassandra Smith, Milwaukee, USA
cassandra-smith.com

Charlene Spiteri (pages 12, 36, 86)
Warp & Weft, Melbourne, Australia
www.warp-weft.com.au

Courtney Kennedy (page 106)
Always Rooney, Oklahome, USA
www.alwaysrooney.com

Elvira Sasso (page 28)
Storelvi, Matera, Italy
www.storelvi.etsy.com

Emma Radke (pages 60, 63, 102)
The Throwbackdaze, Minneapolis, USA
www.etsy.com/shop/thethrowbackdaze

Emilia Lorena (pages 16, 42, 48)
Emilia Lorena, Yamba, New South Wales, Australia
www.emilialorena.com.au

Jo Abellera (page 76)
KKIBO, Los Angeles, USA
kkibo.net

Kirri-Mae Simpson (page 22)
KIRRI-MAdE, Melbourne, Australia
www.etsy.com/au/shop/kirrimaDe

Megan Todd (page 92)
Knots & Knits, Brisbane, Australia
www.knotsandknits.com

Milenka Osen and Georgie Swift of TMOD (page 54)
TMOD, Sydney, Australia
www.tmod.com.au

Tanya Aguiñiga (page 98)
Tanya Aguiñiga Designs, Los Angeles, California
www.aguinigadesign.com

Tino Johnson (pages 112, 117)
Malé, The Maldives

## OTHER CONTRIBUTORS

Anastasia Kazybekava of Thread Design Studio
(page 91)
www.threaddesignstudio.etsy.com

Asmina Fotos of Asmina's Handmade (page 75)
www.etsy.com/shop/asmina

Claudia Rosillo of Texturable (page 105)
www.texturable.com

Erica Fransson of Lillagunilla (page 47)
www.etsy.com/shop/lillagunilla

Erica Maree (page 85)
www.ericamaree.com

Evgenia Garcia of Craft 2 Joy (page 69)
www.etsy.com/uk/shop/craft2joy

Jesika Johnson of Craft Geek (page 111)
www.craftgreekblog.com

Jessica Eden of BohemEden (page 15)
www.etsy.com/shop/BohemEden

Jo Jansen of Buttermilk Design Co (page 91)
www.buttermilkdesignco.com

Julie Comtois of Créations Mariposa (pages 21, 35)
www.creationsmariposa.com

Laura Ayres-Selent of the Vintage Loop
(pages 52, 59, 105)
www.thevintageloop.com

Laura Pifer of Trash to Couture (pages 53, 97)
www.trashtocouture.com

MacK Mars of SoulMakes (page 97)
www.soulmakes.com

Mae Cleary (page 53)
www.knotaday.wordpress.com

Marja and Bea Kort of Passii Sieraden (page 59)
www.etsy.com/shop/PassiiSieraden

Michelle Larson of Beso del Corazon  (page 47)
www.etsy.com/shop/Besodelcorazon

Mingui Kelly (pages 69, 117)
www.etsy.com/shop/MinguiKelly

Paolo Prosperio of the Hang A Hammock
Collective  (page 21)
www.hangahammockcollective.com

Sally England (pages 35, 111)
www.sallyengland.com

Stacey Evans of Sunshine Dreaming (page 41)
www.etsy.com/shop/SunshineDreamingLove

Tato Dobien of Amonithe (page 85)
www.etsy.com/shop/Amonithe

Yuli Fitie (page 27)
www.etsy.com/uk/shop/stoneagetale

## PHOTO CREDITS

Andres Delfino of Estudio Local (page 85, bottom)
www.facebook.com/estudiolocal.ba

Courtney Kennedy of Always Rooney (page 105)
www.alwaysrooney.com

Guy Hamilton of Twofold Creative
(pages 11, 92, 123)
www.twofold.com

Jessica Monnich (page 85, top)
www.lmandbc.com

Milenka Osen and Georgie Swift of TMOD
(page 54)
www.tmod.com.au

Rodrigo Olivera (page 105, bottom)

Image of working board on p9 courtesy
of Beadaholique
www.beadaholique.com

All other photos by Neal Grundy

# Index

# Acknowledgments

Thanks to the talented designers who worked on the project. Your time, patience, and dedication throughout the process are greatly appreciated. This book has benefitted in many ways because of your creative input.

The publishers and editors, Isheeta and Tamsin and my friend Emily Gregory, for helping make this book happen and your ongoing guidance and wisdom throughout.

To my sister, Samantha, and to my parents, Steve and Carol, for providing endless day care, ideas, and ears to bend.

My patient, wonderfully supportive partner, Damon, and my oldest son, Alexander. You have both been my rock, my litmus paper, my late-night support network, my ever-calm weekend saviour. You have picked up the slack time and time again and provided the time and space required to make this book happen. It most definitely would have not been possible without you both. For that, and your ongoing belief in me, I am endlessly grateful. To my soon-to-be-born second son, thanks for giving your mum such an easy pregnancy and allowing her to work right up to your arrival and beyond. We can't wait to meet you.